In Context

Functional Skills English

ENTRY 3 – LEVEL 2

Health & Social Care Workbook

John Meed
Anna Rossetti

Nelson Thornes

This edition published in 2012 by:
Nelson Thornes Ltd
Delta Place
27 Bath Road
CHELTENHAM
GL53 7TH
United Kingdom

13 14 15 16 / 10 9 8 7 6 5 4 3 2

A catalogue record for this book is available from the British Library

ISBN 978 1 4085 1832 8

Cover image: Kudryashka/Shutterstock

Illustrations by James Elston and Paul McCaffrey, Sylvie Poggio Agency

Page make-up by Pantek Media, Maidstone

Printed in China by 1010 Printing International Ltd

Acknowledgements
The authors and the publisher would like to thank the following for permission to reproduce material:

Text
p9 from (www.mencap.co.uk); p15, p17 Health and Safety Executive © Crown Copyright; p19, p21, p79 © Social Care Institute
for Excellence (SCIE); p29 ©2012 About.com. All rights reserved; p35 © WRAP 2012; p39, p41 (Mr Garvey example), p42 Ministry
of Justice © Crown Copyright; p55 produced by kind permission of the Department of Health, © 2012; p59 © Local Government
Improvement and Development 2001–2010; p69 Copyright © 2012 Hearing Advisor; p71 both extracts taken from (www.amazon.
co.uk); p85 © 2012 Young Minds; p87 © 2011 Public Health Agency; p89 adapted 'Health and Safety in Care Homes' by HSE
© Crown Copyright; p95 from 'Does illness and old age have to mean crap food?' Copyright Guardian News and Media Ltd 2012;
p97 © Copyright 2012 Wiltshire Farm Foods. All rights reserved; p99 DirectGov © Crown Copyright; p105 Office of Fair Trading
© Crown Copyright; p107 taken from Bank Safe Online (www.banksafeonline.ork.uk); p109 taken from Aviva Equity Release
brochure (www.aviva.co.uk); p111 (top quote) © Age UK Group and/or its National Partners (Age NI, Age Scotland, Age Cymru)
2012. All rights reserved; p111 (middle quote) taken from Money Saving Expert (www.moneysavingexpert.com) p111 (bottom
quote) from 'Should I consider equity release?' Copyright Guardian News and Media Ltd 2006.
All Crown Copyright material is reproduced under PSI licence no. C2009002012.

Images
Alamy: p14 (David Levenson), p15 (Paul Doyle), p19 (Jack Sullivan), p28 (Oredia), p35 (Justin Kase z11z), p55 (Martin
Turzak), p69 (Ron Chapple Stock), p84 (Paul Doyle), p109 (MBI), p115cl (Andrew Maynard); Care Images: p115br; Heart n Soul:
p59; iStockphoto: p71tr (Rolf Weschke); Mencap: p9; Phonak nano: p71cr; Photofusion: p29 (Crispin Hughes), p49 (John Birdsall),
p52 (Paula Solloway), p89 (Jacky Chapman); Press Association Images: p5 (Tim Ireland), p119 (Dave Chidley/The Canadian Press);
Topfoto: p45 (Socialstock).

Every effort has been made to trace the copyright holders but if any have been inadvertently overlooked the publisher will be
pleased to make the necessary arrangements at the first opportunity.

Contents

Introduction

"Functional skills are the fundamental, applied skills in English, mathematics, and information and communication technology (ICT) which help people to gain the most from life, learning and work."

Ofqual (2012), Criteria for Functional Skills Qualifications

This workbook is designed to present functional English in a variety of contexts to make it accessible and relevant to you, as Health and Social Care candidates. It is intended to be written in, so use it as a record of your progress!

Being 'functional' means that you will:

- be able to apply skills to all sorts of real-life contexts
- have the mental ability to take on challenges in a range of new settings
- be able to work independently
- realise that tasks often need persistence, thought and reflection.

Features of this workbook are:

 **Source**

These pages will cover important aspects of Health and Social Care and consist of some interesting source materials, such as newspaper articles or industry-related information, followed by various questions and activities for you to complete.

 **FOCUS ON**

Each Focus on is typically 1–2 pages long and will teach you specific Functional Skills. They include:

- guidance on the skill
- one or more activities to practise the skill.

Good luck!

'Inhumane abuse'

Ministers stepped in after police arrested four people following a BBC *Panorama* documentary showing the 'inhumane abuse' of adults with learning difficulties and autism. The home is funded by the taxpayer and costs £3,500 a week.

Undercover filming showed patients at Winterbourne View in Bristol being pinned down, slapped, doused in cold water and repeatedly taunted and teased.

Care services minister Paul Burstow ordered a 'thorough examination' of the role of the Care Quality Commission and local authorities after a whistleblower's claims about the home were not followed up. He said: 'There can be no place for such inhumanity in care services. There have been failures of inspection and adult protection which have exposed people to appalling abuse.'

The Care Quality Commission apologised and said in a statement: 'We apologise to those who have been let down by our failure to act more swiftly to address the appalling treatment that people at this hospital were subjected to.'

Mark Goldring, chief executive of learning disability charity Mencap, said the treatment of patients was 'like torture' and called for the hospital to be closed down. 'The behaviour of the individuals was cruel and barbaric and the management seemed to be either complicit or non-existent.'

Lee Reed, chief executive of care provider Castlebeck which runs the home, said he would 'leave no stone unturned to ensure that this type of horrific event is never allowed to happen again.'

A In a group, discuss these questions. Make notes here.

1 Have you heard about this story?

2 Have you heard about other similar stories?

3 What do you think about it?

4 How can abuse like this happen?

B Write down what each of these words means.

1	Inhumane	
2	Autism	
3	Whistleblower	
4	Barbaric	
5	Documentary	
6	Complicit	

C Write down answers to these questions.

1 Who does the home cater for?

2 Give two examples of the abuse.

a)

b)

3 How much does the home cost?

4 How was the abuse discovered?

D Who said what?

1	'There can be no place for such inhumanity in care services.'	
2	'We apologise to those who have been let down by our failure to act'	
3	'the management seemed to be either complicit or non-existent.'	
4	He would 'leave no stone unturned to ensure that this type of horrific event is never allowed to happen again.'	

E Work with a partner. Add capital letters and full stops to these sentences.

1 ministers stepped in after police arrested four people following a bbc *panorama* documentary

2 undercover filming showed patients at winterbourne view in bristol

3 care services minister paul burstow ordered a 'thorough examination' of the role of the care quality commission

F Fill in the gaps in this paragraph. Insert words that make sense.

Adults with learning _____ should be treated with care and respect. They deserve high _____ of care. It is _____ to hear of abuse like this. It is important to pay _____ to claims from whistleblowers. The Care _____ Commission is responsible for inspecting services in _____ and, in this case, they clearly _____. They must make sure that nothing like this ever _____ again.

G Work with a partner. Discuss three ways in which abuse like this could be prevented in the future. You could make notes here.

1

2

3

H Write a short letter to the paper. Aim for three paragraphs about:

- how you heard about the abuse at Winterbourne View
- your reaction to reading about it
- what you think should be done.

| | (Your address) |

(The paper's address)

| (Date) |

Dear

Yours sincerely/faithfully

(Your signature)

SOURCE **Charity and celebrities**

Many of the health and social care charities in the UK benefit from celebrity support. This raises awareness of the charity and its work and helps to raise a great deal of money.

Celebrity support for Mencap

Mencap works with people with a learning disability to change laws, challenge prejudice and support them to live their lives as they choose. Everything we do is about valuing and supporting people with a learning disability, and their families and carers. Mencap has a number of Celebrity Ambassadors who support their work.

The Edge was invited to become an ambassador by his cousin Ciara Evans, who works for Mencap and has a learning disability.

He says: *'Not many people know what a learning disability is, or the challenges people with a learning disability face. I've seen how much work goes into Mencap and want to continue to see it flourish.'*

Christopher Eccleston researched the subject in great depth for his first major film role, in which he played a character with a learning disability.

He says: *'I'd like to increase the visibility of people with a learning disability in drama.'*

Lisa Scott-Lee became an ambassador for Mencap as a 'tribute' to her two uncles, Alex and Andreas, both of whom have a learning disability.

She says: *'Learning disability is still a taboo subject in the media. One of the main things I can do as a celebrity is raise awareness and help create a greater understanding.'*

Will Young is an incredibly active supporter of the charity. He recently gave the proceeds from one his Arena tours to Mencap and regularly performs at Mencap events.

He says: *'I like the fact that Mencap helps to empower people by giving them their own home and enabling them to work so they don't feel so helpless and victimised ... I feel I am very much in this for the long term and I'd like to continue to break down people's misconceptions and prejudices about learning disability.'*

Jo Whiley became an ambassador for Mencap because her sister Frances has a condition called Cri du Chat syndrome. Jo uses her contacts in the music industry, and her reputation as a champion of new talent, to attract a wealth of stars to the charity's week-long indoor acoustic music festival.

A In a group, discuss these questions.

1 Have you heard of Mencap?

2 Do you know what it does?

3 Do you think it is important to have a charity like this?

B For each of the following words, write a sentence that contains the word.

1 Taboo

2 Flourish

3 Visibility

4 Empower

5 Prejudice

C Read the text and answer these questions.

1 Who wants to see Mencap flourish?

2 Why did Lisa Scott-Lee become a Mencap ambassador?

3 Which actor found out about learning disability for a film role?

4 How does Will Young support Mencap?

5 How does Jo Whiley use contacts in the music industry to help Mencap?

6 According to Will Young, how does Mencap empower people?

7 Which three celebrities talk about the importance of helping people to understand learning disability?

D Do you agree with the opinions below?

1 Lisa Scott-Lee says that 'learning disability is still a taboo subject in the media.'

Do you agree? Why?

2 Christopher Eccleston says that he would like to 'increase the visibility of people with a learning disability in drama.'

Do you agree this is necessary? Why?

E With a partner, discuss these questions.

1 Which of these celebrities have you heard of?

2 Do you think that celebrity support is important to charities?

3 Why might a celebrity become involved?

4 How can they help?

5 What celebrities do you know of who support other charities?

F Draft an email to a celebrity of your choice persuading them to support a charity.

1 Introduce yourself and explain why you are writing.

2 Outline briefly what the charity does.

3 Say how the celebrity could support the charity.

4 Share your email with a partner.

| Message | Adobe PDF |

Reply Reply Forward Delete Move to Create Other Block Not Junk Safe Lists Categorize Follow Mark as Select Find Related Send to OneNote
       to All   Folder Rule Actions Sender   Up Unread

Respond   Actions   Junk E-mail   Options   Find   OneNote

To:

Subject:

FOCUS ON **Proper nouns**

Sentences start with a capital letter, but capital letters are also used for proper nouns. Proper nouns are the names of a specific or unique:

* person
* place
* organisation
* item or brand.

Days of the week and months also have capitals (e.g. Monday, July), as do titles such as Mr, Mrs and Ms.

They are different from common nouns, which do not have capitals.

Here are some examples:

Common noun	Proper noun
person	Ms Ayisha Khan
city	Bristol
country	France
care home	Ocean View
organisation	Mencap
bed brand	Slumberland
place	Regent's Park

 A Four of these words are proper nouns. Which ones are they?

* Lizzie
* Temperature
* Visitor
* Oxford
* Hazard
* Castlebeck
* Alzheimer's
* Dementia

B The sentences below have no capital letters in them. Underline each word that should start with a capital letter.

1 mr paul stevens is the manager of the green hill care home.

2 julie is a care assistant and works on friday, saturday and sunday.

3 the clients had tea in snowdrop tea rooms.

4 sonia will take her holiday in july.

5 the care quality commission is based in newcastle.

6 there are many residential care homes in bournemouth.

7 the supported-living flat was equipped with a bosch dishwasher.

8 the lunch menu gave a choice of roast chicken or macaroni cheese.

9 the royal college of nursing is a national organisation that supports nurses.

10 the residents were taken to pizza express on the day trip.

C Give an example of a proper noun for each category below.

1 Town

2 Equipment

3 Company

4 Brand

5 Person

6 Place

Handle with care!

In health and social care, moving and positioning injuries account for 40 per cent of work-related sickness absence. Around 5,000 moving and positioning injuries are reported each year in health services and around 2,000 in social care.

Moving and positioning is a key part of the working day for most care workers; from moving equipment, laundry, catering, supplies or waste to assisting individuals in moving. Poor moving and positioning practice can lead to:

- back pain and other injuries – which may mean time off work
- moving and positioning accidents – which can injure the client and care worker
- discomfort and a lack of dignity for the client.

Over 50 per cent of injuries arise from moving and positioning people. Activities that may increase the risk include moving individuals, assisting in treatment and helping with daily activities such as bathing.

The law says employers must take action to prevent or minimise the risk of injury. It is important to assess the risks for each client, finding out:

- what the client is able/unable to do independently
- how well the client can support their own weight

- other relevant factors such as pain, disability or tendency to fall
- how well the client can participate in/ cooperate with moves
- whether the client needs help to reposition themselves (e.g. sit up)
- what equipment may be needed (e.g. hoists)
- how many staff are needed to ensure safe moves.

It is then possible to take steps to reduce the risks, where possible involving the client or their family in planning how to meet their needs. These measures are then recorded in a risk assessment form that all staff should follow.

A True or false?

Which of these statements are true and which are false, according to the text?

1 2,000 moving and positioning injuries are reported each year in social care.
   True ☐   False ☐

2 20 per cent of work-related sickness absence arises from moving and positioning injuries.
   True ☐   False ☐

3 Moving and positioning accidents can injure the client and the care worker.
   True ☐   False ☐

4 Where possible, involve the client or their family in planning how to meet their needs.
   True ☐   False ☐

B Write down answers to these questions.

1 Who is this text written for?

2 What is the purpose of the text?

3 Give two examples of problems that can be caused by manual positioning.

a) [   ]

b) [   ]

4 Give two examples of activities that have manual positioning risks.

a) [   ]

b) [   ]

5 What does the law say employers must do about this?

C Read this short description of a real case study.

Washing with care

Mr G had multiple sclerosis and was cared for by two workers. He weighed 75 kg, had full use of his arms and hands but little strength in his legs and feet. The care workers would wash Mr G while he was in bed. One care worker would roll Mr G towards her and the second would wash his back. The carer holding Mr G suffered lower back pain as a result.

D With a partner, discuss these questions.

1 Have you had any experiences like the one described?

2 What happened?

3 What was done to reduce the risks?

 E How well did you listen to each other while discussing the questions?

Give yourselves a score for each statement below:

- Score 3 if this was true most of the time.
- Score 2 if this was sometimes true.
- Score 1 if this did not happen very often.

	Statement	Score (3–1)
1	We took turns to speak.	
2	We listened carefully when the other person spoke.	
3	We looked at each other often while we were talking.	
4	We avoided interrupting each other.	
5	We showed when we agreed, e.g. by nodding, saying 'yes'.	
6	We asked questions to check we had understood.	

F Note down two things you could do another time to make sure you listen carefully to each other.

1

2

G Write two paragraphs about a client you know.

Describe the help they need that involves moving and positioning.

Describe how you can minimise the risks of injury for them and for you.

FIVE EXAMPLES OF BEST PRACTICE

The Social Care Institute for Excellence (SCIE) describes several ways in which health and social care organisations seek to ensure that clients eat with dignity.

Hyndburn

During induction at Hyndburn Short Break Service for people with learning disabilities, staff spend time with the person, their family and any other professionals involved to establish the person's dietary requirements, preferences, usual routines and any individual guidelines. Before the person's stay, staff use their person-centred meal plan and ensure their preferences are included in shopping for that week. Main meals are eaten around a table in a 'family' atmosphere and staff support individuals who require assistance.

Leicestershire

The Leicestershire Home Care Assessment and Reablement team has had success in motivating people to start cooking again. For example, an ex-miner had never made himself a cup of tea or cooked a meal. When his wife died his family thought he would be unable to cope. The team encouraged him to use the kettle and the microwave and to make simple meals – starting with beans on toast. They encouraged him to go out and he now has his main meal in a local café. He is coping well, to the surprise and delight of his family.

University Hospitals Bristol

On one ward of the University Hospitals Bristol NHS Foundation Trust a 'volunteers and mealtime' project provides more assistance to elderly patients. Volunteers help to make mealtimes a more social occasion. Each volunteer attends a multi-professional half-day training programme.

St Michael's Community Hospital

In St Michael's Community Hospital, Aylsham, the ward housekeeper, together with a healthcare assistant, spoke to patients about mealtime practices and asked for ideas as to how they could be improved. Following patients' suggestions, mealtimes were protected and made more of an event, with new cutlery and tablecloths improving the dining environment. Since the changes were made, patients have reported enjoying mealtimes more.

Southampton University Hospitals

At Southampton University Hospitals NHS Trust, a 'nutritional awareness week' helped raise the understanding of how important it is for patients to receive good nutritional food. Guidance was also given to all wards on nutritional supplements.

A Match the action to the organisation.

Which organisation has tried out each of these actions?

Organisation
1 Leicestershire Home Care Assessment and Reablement Team
2 St Michael's Community Hospital
3 University Hospitals Bristol
4 Hyndburn Short Break Service
5 Southampton University Hospitals

Action
a) A nutritional awareness week
b) Person-centred meal plan
c) Motivating people to start cooking again
d) Speaking to patients about mealtime practices
e) Volunteers and mealtimes project

B Write down answers to these questions.

1 How do staff at Hyndburn use the person-centred meal plan?

2 What did the Leicestershire team encourage the ex-miner to do?

3 What changes did the St Michael's ward housekeeper make?

4 How did University Hospitals Bristol make mealtimes a more social occasion?

C In your group discuss eating with dignity. You could make notes below.

1 Which of the actions described seem most useful to you?

2 How do the care organisations that you know approach eating?

3 What improvements might you be able to suggest?

D Read this fact sheet.

social care
institute for excellence

Dignity in Care factsheet

June 2010

Eating and nutritional care in practice

- Carry out routine nutritional screening when admitting people to hospital or residential care. Record the dietary needs and preferences of individuals and any assistance they need at mealtimes and ensure staff act on this.

- Refer the person for professional assessment if screening raises particular concerns.

- Make food look appetising. Not all food for people with swallowing difficulties needs to be puréed. Keep different foods separate to enhance the quality of the eating experience.

- Make sure food is available and accessible between mealtimes.

- Give people time to eat; they should not be rushed.

- Provide assistance discreetly to people who have difficulty eating. Use serviettes, not bibs, to protect clothing.

- While socialising during mealtimes should be encouraged, offer privacy to those who have difficulties with eating, if they wish.

- Ensure that mealtimes are sufficiently staffed to provide assistance to those who need it. If there are insufficient staff, introduce a system of staggered mealtimes.

- Encourage carers, family and friends to visit and offer support at mealtimes.

Hydration

- Encourage people to drink regularly throughout the day. The Food Standards Agency recommends a daily intake of six to eight glasses of water or other fluids.

- Provide education, training and information about the benefits of good hydration to staff, carers and people who use services.

- Ensure there is access to clean drinking water 24 hours a day.

- If people are reluctant to drink water, think of other ways of increasing their fluid intake, for example with alternative drinks and foods that have a higher fluid content, (eg breakfast cereals with milk, soup, and fruit and vegetables).

- If people show reluctance to drink because they are worried about incontinence, reassure them that help will be provided with going to the toilet. It may help some people to avoid drinking before bedtime.

- Be aware of urine colour as an indication of hydration level (Water UK, 2005); odourless, pale urine indicates good hydration. Dark, strong-smelling urine could be an indicator of poor hydration – but there may be other causes that should be investigated.

Ideas you could use

Ask people how their mealtimes could be improved

Ask the people who use your service for their ideas about improving mealtimes – and put their suggestions into practice.

Recruit volunteers to improve mealtimes

Create a pool of volunteers to help make mealtimes more sociable and assist people with eating where needed.

To find out more, visit SCIE's Dignity in care guide at **www.scie.org.uk**

E Write five sentences using one of these words in each sentence.

1 Screening

2 Hydration

3 Intake

4 Appetising

5 Nutrition

F Write down answers to these questions about hydration.

1 Give one way you can help people who do not want to drink water.

2 What is the recommended daily fluid intake?

3 What can you do if someone is worried about drinking because of incontinence?

4 What urine signs may indicate poor hydration?

G With a partner, draft a checklist of ideas to help people eat with dignity.

FOCUS ON Apostrophes

There are two ways in which we use apostrophes:

- When letters are missing
- To show possession

Apostrophes to show that letters are missing

When we deliberately shorten a word or phrase we can use an apostrophe to show that letters are missing. This is also called a 'contraction'.

We use an apostrophe when two words are combined to make one

- For example: 'I am' is shortened to 'I'm'.

A Replace the words in brackets with one word containing an apostrophe.

1 (He is) ⬚ working with people with learning disabilities.

2 We will not be able to visit next week because (we are) ⬚ busy.

3 (They are) ⬚ going to come on Tuesday.

We often use an apostrophe to shorten 'have' or 'has'

- For example: 'we have' is shortened to 'we've'.

B Replace the words in brackets with one word containing an apostrophe.

1 His wife (was not) ⬚ able to visit today.

2 We (were not) ⬚ expecting the gas engineer.

3 We (cannot) ⬚ take any more residents at the moment.

4 I (could not) ⬚ believe how much food was thrown away.

5 The council (would not) ⬚ collect the old mattress.

6 Why (do not) ⬚ you spend more time with the clients?

Note: People often confuse 'you're' and 'your'. 'You're' is short for 'you are', while 'your' means 'belonging to you'. Similarly, 'they're' is short for 'they are', while 'there' is a place. If you are not sure, say it in full.

C Replace the words in brackets with one word containing an apostrophe.

1 (I have) ⬚ found a good place to buy local vegetables.

2 (They have) ⬚ gone away for two weeks.

3 Dave has given me a leaflet that (he has) ⬚ written about hydration.

The word 'not' is often shortened to 'n't' when it is combined with another word

- For example: 'is not' is shortened to 'isn't'.

The possessive apostrophe

A lot of people are confused by the possessive apostrophe. Some people try to overcome the problem by putting an apostrophe after any 's' at the end of a word but this is incorrect.

It is called the possessive apostrophe because it is used when writing about something that belongs to, or is owned by, a person, place or thing.

An apostrophe followed by 's' ('s) is added to singular words (i.e. where there is only one person, place or thing)

- For example: my neighbour's bin = the bin belonging to my neighbour.

D Put the apostrophe in the correct place below.

Her friends old clothes. (One friend)

If the word is plural and already ends with an 's', then you just add an apostrophe at the end of the word (i.e. after the 's')

- For example: her friends' old clothes = the old clothes belonging to her friends. (More than one friend)

E Put the apostrophe in the correct place below.

The boys room. (More than one boy)

An apostrophe followed by 's' ('s) is added to plural words that do not end with an 's'

- For example: the children's toys = the toys belonging to the children.

F Put the apostrophe in the correct place below.

The mens equipment.

SOURCE How your memory works

The brain

Your brain is like an amazing computer that stores memories and information. There are two types of memory.

Short-term memory holds a small amount of information for a short period of time. It makes particular use of the part of your brain called the 'pre-frontal lobe'.

Long-term memory stores an unlimited amount of information indefinitely.

Information is transferred from short-term to long-term memory

Facts

- Brains never become full, but they do forget if you do not exercise them.
- Your memory is more likely to remember things that are important or that form a pattern.
- Different parts of the same memory are stored in different parts of your brain.
- Most human beings find handwriting, speech and faces easy to remember.

cortex

pre-frontal lobe

hippocampus

through a special part of the brain. This part of the brain, called the 'hippocampus', is like a sorting centre where new sensations are compared with previous ones.

When we remember new facts by repeating them or using other memory techniques we are actually passing them through the hippocampus several times. This keeps strengthening the associations among these new elements until the brain has learned to associate these things to create what we call a memory.

The hippocampus is important in what is called **episodic memory**. This lets you remember something years later, like a happy holiday. It allows you to 'play the scene back' by restarting the pattern of the activity in the various parts of the brain.

How to improve your memory

Here are some tips on how to improve your memory:

- **Repetition:** this is the best way to remember things for a short period of time, such as a phone number or ingredients for a recipe.
- **Make up a story:** if you have to remember a list of things, create a story that includes them all. This will make connections between them and you will remember them better.
- **Mental exercise:** games, puzzles and mental arithmetic are like 'brain aerobics'.
- **Physical exercise:** this increases your heart rate and sends more oxygen to your brain, which makes your memory work better.
- **Listen to music:** research shows that listening to relaxing instrumental music helps you to organise ideas more clearly and remember things better.
- **Eat the right things:** food containing omega-3, such as fish, spinach and olive oil, helps to improve your memory. Vitamins C and E (in oranges, strawberries and red grapes) and vitamin B (in meat and green vegetables) are also good for your brain.
- **Control stress:** relaxing, getting enough sleep and positive thinking also help your memory.

A Read the text and answer these questions.

1 What type of memory stores information for a short period?

2 Which part of the brain compares previous sensations with new ones?

3 Name one type of thing that human beings find easy to remember.

4 What is the best way to remember things for a short time?

5 What sends more oxygen to the brain and makes your memory work better?

6 Name a food that contains omega-3.

B What do you remember or forget?

1 Make a note of what you need to remember:

a) at home.

b) at college.

c) at work.

2 What do you do to help you remember?

3 What do you tend to forget?

Share your list with a partner.

C Spend 30 seconds looking at the list of 20 words on page 28 and try to remember as many as you can.

Now write all of the words that you remember here.

If you remembered at least five, that is good.

What methods did you use to remember them?

Did you try making up a story to connect the words?

D Look at the words you wrote down. Did you spell them all correctly?

Jot down here any that you got wrong and try to learn them. Then have another go.

E Write a story to help you remember these words.

work   sandwich   hat   empty   pink   inside   shirt   angry   umbrella   fly

F I went on holiday.

This is a group game for 4 to 10 players.

The first person says, 'I went on holiday and I took …'

They follow this by saying something they might take on holiday, for example, sunglasses.

The second person says, 'I went on holiday and I took sunglasses and …', adding another item, such as a beach towel.

Each person has to remember all of the things that have been said before and add a new one at the end.

If someone forgets an item then they have to drop out.

Play goes on until only one person is left.

Words to remember for C:

fish	blue	five	hand	bucket
sad	today	tall	dress	why
banana	eat	boat	tree	silly
fiddlesticks	wall	star	chair	sleep

SOURCE Keeping fit with age

Getting older and gaining weight

It is true that getting older can often involve losing muscle and gaining fat, but it does not have to be that way. Exercise can help people to stay fit, healthy and avoid weight gain as they get older.

The reason for gaining weight is not connected just to getting older, it is about how habits change. Many older people gain weight because they:

- become more sedentary
- lift less weight to maintain muscle mass
- eat more calories even though their metabolism has slowed down.

What can help?

The main reason for muscle loss is that, as people get older, they often spend too much time sitting down – at work, when watching TV and when using the computer. This slows down their metabolism. Being active and lifting weights helps to preserve muscle and increase bone density while maintaining a faster metabolism.

Before starting on an exercise programme, the person should see their doctor. Then, once they have clearance to exercise, they can follow this basic approach to getting fit.

Cardio exercise

They should choose an activity they like, such as swimming, walking or cycling, and try to do that activity at least three days a week. They should start gently and gradually add time until they can do 30 minutes of exercise each time.

Lift weights

Strength training can be one of the most important parts of an exercise programme. It builds muscle and strength while also working on important areas, such as balance, stability and flexibility – all things that tend to decline with age.

A healthy diet

A good diet for older people will include plenty of whole grains, fruits and vegetables. They also need to watch their calorie intake.

Be realistic

As people get older, it will take longer to lose weight, so it helps to focus on doing the workouts and eating as healthily as possible. If an older person does that, then their body will respond in its own time.

A Write down what each of these words means.

1	Sedentary	
2	Metabolism	

B Read the text and answer these questions.

1 What should an older person do before they start an exercise programme?

2 What type of activity helps with balance?

3 What effect does a sedentary lifestyle have on the body?

4 Give two examples of cardio exercise.

5 Name three things that older people should include in their diet.

C Fill each gap below with a word so that the text makes sense.

As people get older they often put on [   ]. One of the reasons for this is that they spend too much [   ] sitting down. This [   ] their metabolism. Being active and [   ] weights increases their bone [   ] and preserves [   ]. They should also try to do a [   ] activity at least three times a [   ].

D Think of an older person you know. They can be someone you work with or a member of your family.

Write a short case study of them, including details of their weight, general health and any exercise they take. Remember to change their name to retain confidentiality.

Share your case study with a small group.

E Add full stops and capital letters to the case study below.

mrs adams is 66 years old she became depressed after her husband

died and spends most of her day watching television she has put on a

lot of weight which makes her breathless when she goes to the shops

her gp referred her to the local gym where she has joined an exercise

group for older people she says 'i love going to the gym and i feel fitter

already everyone is very nice and i've made some new friends'

F   Work with a partner to plan a poster aimed at older people to show them the benefits of exercise.

G   Answer the following questions using a complete sentence.

1   What might prevent an older person taking more exercise?

2   How could you encourage an older person to get more exercise?

Share your ideas with the whole group.

FOCUS ON Non-verbal communication

Non-verbal communication (NVC) is any type of behaviour that is not speech. It is a very powerful communication tool. We are often unaware of the NVC we use.

NVC can be as important as what we say when we are speaking or listening to another person. The NVC used by health and social care staff can make a big difference to the quality of a client's experience.

Being conscious of one's own NVC, and being able to interpret that of others, can help us to understand ourselves and others better.

NVC includes:

- body language
- vocal signals
- personal presentation.

Body language includes a wide range of things such as facial expression, gestures with hands, arms or legs, posture and eye contact.

Vocal signals mean the tone or pitch of your voice when speaking as well as sounds such as 'Mmmm', 'Aha' and 'Er'. These show that you are listening.

A Think about how a health and social care worker can use NVC positively when interacting with clients. Write your ideas for each type of NVC.

1 Facial expression

2 Gestures

3 Posture

4 Eye contact

5 Tone of voice

B Match each form of NVC to its possible meaning.

NVC		Possible meaning	
1	Sitting with arms crossed	a)	Agreement
2	Tight lips	b)	Open and welcoming
3	Raised eyebrows	c)	'I do not understand'
4	Slumped in a chair	d)	Bored, not interested
5	Raised voice	e)	Disagreement
6	Arms by sides, relaxed posture	f)	Rejection, defensive
7	Walking with head up	g)	Disbelief or sarcasm
8	Nodding	h)	Anger or fear
9	'Er ...'	i)	Confident

A word of warning!

You will have realised already that, while NVC is helpful in understanding others' unspoken thoughts and feelings, we should be careful about how we interpret it.

For example, you may work with clients whose NVC is affected by health or impairment issues. For example, facial expressions may be different in someone who has suffered a stroke.

C Can you think of two examples of how a client's health or impairment could affect their NVC?

1

2

D Look at the examples of NVC below. Circle the ones that you think you use frequently.

touching your nose   hands clasped behind head

smiling   tapping fingers   crossing arms

crossing legs   standing up straight

nodding   frowning   avoiding eye contact

making eye contact   hands on hips

tight or pursed lips

Ask a friend if they agree with you.

No more waste

Plans have been drawn up to build a new health and social care centre at a cost of approximately £7m. Before starting construction, a cost and benefit analysis was carried out to improve waste management. This is important in two ways:

- It is good for the environment as it will mean that less waste goes to landfill.
- It can save costs in building the health centre.

The health centre will be built on the site of a primary school which is about to be demolished. It will be a large building, three storeys high. The study found that there was a potential saving of £22,985 if the waste reduction plan was implemented.

The study identified the top opportunities for reducing, reusing and recycling waste and estimated how much could be saved from implementing these measures.

Construction materials are a valuable resource. But often there are high levels of waste through things such as damage on the site, ordering too many materials and the need to redo work if it is not done properly. Reducing this waste saves money.

Waste disposal also costs money. The less waste you have, the less you need to dispose of. Segregating waste into different types and finding destinations other than landfill will save money. The analysis found that using three skips instead of one, and segregating waste, could save £13,630 of the cost of building the health centre.

Reducing waste to save money

No one wants money to be spent unnecessarily. In the healthcare sector, money saved on costs such as building could be used to improve or add to services.

These were the recommendations from the analysis about how to save money:

- The client needs to instruct the designers of the building to look for waste reduction opportunities.
- The designers need to look for opportunities to design out waste, for example by simplifying the specification.
- The amount of waste produced should be reduced by strategies such as avoiding ordering and reducing offcuts.
- The cost of waste disposal can be reduced, firstly by producing less waste and also by finding ways to avoid waste going to landfill.
- The waste management contractor must ensure that the waste they receive is recycled wherever possible.

A Choose the correct answer each time.

1 On which site is the new health and social care centre being built?

    a) A landfill site ☐

    b) An old primary school site ☐

    c) A waste management site ☐

2 Using three skips instead of one and segregating waste could save:

    a) £13,630 ☐

    b) £22,630 ☐

    c) £22,985 ☐

3 How can designers design out waste?

    a) Recycling waste ☐

    b) Simplifying the specification ☐

    c) Redoing work that is not done properly ☐

4 What should the waste management contractor ensure?

    a) Waste reduction opportunities are identified ☐

    b) Ordering and offcuts are reduced ☐

    c) The waste they receive is recycled wherever possible ☐

B Write down answers to these questions.

1 How much will it cost to build the new health and social care centre?

2 What are the two reasons why the cost and benefit analysis is important?

a)

b)

3 Give two examples of waste of construction materials.

a)

b)

4 How can the money saved on building be spent?

C In your group discuss waste. You could make notes below.

1 How do the care organisations that you know reduce waste?

2 How might they be able to reduce waste further?

D With a partner, decide where to put commas into these sentences.

1 Before starting construction a cost and benefit analysis was carried out.

2 The less waste you have the less you need to dispose of.

3 Using three skips instead of one to segregate waste could save £13,630.

4 Ways of reducing waste include designing out waste simplifying the specification and reducing offcuts.

5 Care homes can help the environment by ordering only what they need buying products with less packaging creating less waste and recycling more.

E Fill the gaps in these sentences using the following words:

compost   paper   packaging   facility   charity   disposable

1 Give old clothes to a [   ] shop.

2 Take waste to a local recycling [   ].

3 You can make [   ] from fruit and vegetable peelings.

4 You can reduce waste by buying food with less [   ].

5 Make sure that old newspapers go in the [   ] recycling bin.

6 Purchase things you can use again rather than [   ] items.

F Draw a mind map here to show ways of reducing waste in health and social care.

Mind maps are a good way of organising the main points for a piece of writing. To create a mind map, write the topic in the centre of the page (for this example, it is 'Reducing waste') and then draw lines to join it to other ideas (e.g. recycling). You can add further lines and detail.

Reducing waste

G Use your mind map to help you draft a one-sided leaflet about reducing waste in health and social care.

The 'statutory principles'

Mental capacity is 'the ability to make a decision about a particular matter at the time the decision needs to be made'.

The Mental Capacity Act 2005 is the legal framework for acting and making decisions on behalf of individuals who do not have the mental capacity to make particular decisions for themselves.

Everyone working with and/or caring for an adult who may lack capacity to make specific decisions must comply with the 2005 Act. The same rules apply whether the decisions are life-changing events or everyday matters.

The Act is intended to enable and support people, not to restrict or control their lives. It aims to protect people who lack the capacity to make particular decisions. It is also designed to maximise their ability to make decisions, or to participate in decision-making, as far as they are able to do so.

Section 1 of the Act sets out the five 'statutory principles' – these are the values that underpin the Act. The five statutory principles are:

1 **A person must be assumed to have capacity unless it is established that they lack capacity**. Every adult has the right to make their own decisions if they have the capacity to do so. Family carers and healthcare or social care staff must assume that a person has the capacity to make decisions unless it can be established that they do not.

2 **A person is not to be treated as unable to make a decision unless all practicable steps to help them to do so have been taken without success**. People should receive support to help them make their own decisions. Before concluding that individuals lack capacity to make a particular decision, it is important to take all possible steps to try to help them reach a decision themselves.

3 **A person is not to be treated as unable to make a decision merely because they make an unwise decision**. People have the right to make decisions that others might think are unwise. A person who makes a decision that others think is unwise should not automatically be labelled as lacking the capacity to make a decision.

4 An action taken, or decision made, for or on behalf of a person who lacks capacity **must be done or made in their best interests**.

5 Before the action is taken, or the decision is made, thought must be given to whether the purpose can be achieved in a way that is **less restrictive of the person's rights and freedom of action**.

A Find this information in the text and write it down.

1 What is 'mental capacity'?

2 Which Act sets the legal framework for mental capacity?

3 Who must comply with this Act?

4 Who does the Act protect?

5 What are the five rules called that set out the basic values of the Act?

B Here are the five 'statutory principles' but with words missing. Choose the right word from the list to fill each gap.

unwise   restrictive   practicable   behalf   freedom   established

1 A person must be assumed to have capacity unless it is ( ) that they lack capacity.

2 A person is not to be treated as unable to make a decision unless all ( ) steps to help them to do so have been taken without success.

3 A person is not to be treated as unable to make a decision merely because they make an ( ) decision.

4 An act done, or decision made, for or on ( ) of a person who lacks capacity must be done or made in their best interests.

5 Before the act is done, or the decision is made, thought must be given to whether the purpose can be achieved in a way that is less ( ) of the person's rights and ( ) of action.

C Match each of these 'statutory principles' to the relevant example.

Statutory principle	Example
1 A person must be assumed to have capacity unless it is established that they lack capacity.	a) Mr Garvey has mental health problems and sees a community psychiatric nurse regularly. He decides to spend £3,000 of his savings on a camper van to travel round Scotland. The nurse is worried that he may not get the support he needs.
2 A person is not to be treated as unable to make a decision unless all practicable steps to help them to do so have been taken without success.	b) Mrs Arnold has dementia. Her son is worried that she is becoming confused about money. He spends time with her and finds that she can cope with day-to-day things such as shopping but not more difficult financial decisions.
3 A person is not to be treated as unable to make a decision merely because they make an unwise decision.	c) Mr Jackson is in hospital after a traffic accident. He needs urgent treatment but is in distress and cannot speak. A nurse recognises some gestures as sign language. When she starts signing to him he becomes calmer.

D In a group discuss this case study.

Sara, a young woman with severe depression, is getting treatment from mental health services.

Her mother is trying to persuade Sara to agree to electroconvulsive therapy (ECT), which helped her own mother when she had clinical depression in the past.

A friend has told Sara that ECT is 'barbaric'.

Her psychiatrist believes Sara can make decisions about treatment if she gets advice and support.

1 Spend two to three minutes reading the case study and thinking about what you will say.

2 Spend a few minutes discussing the issues raised.

3 What needs to happen to make sure that Sara is involved in the decisions about her treatment?

You could try taking on the roles of the different people and discussing the issues from their points of view.

Use this space to make any notes you need.

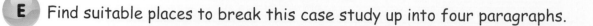

E Find suitable places to break this case study up into four paragraphs.

Jane has a learning disability. She expresses herself using some words, facial expressions and body language. However, she finds it difficult to discuss abstract ideas or things she has not experienced. She has lived in her current community home all her life, but now needs to move to a new group home. Staff are concerned that she may not be able to decide for herself which new group home she should move to. The staff ask an advocate to help Jane express her views. Jane's advocate uses pictures, symbols and Makaton to find out the things that are important to Jane and speaks to people who know Jane to find out what they think she likes. She then supports Jane to show their work to her care manager and discuss Jane's needs and preferences. When the care manager has found some suitable places, Jane and her advocate visit the homes together. They take photos of the houses and then use the photos to help Jane work out which home she prefers. Jane's own feelings can now play an important part in deciding where she will live.

F Work with a partner to prepare a one-page leaflet for colleagues. Your leaflet should explain what they need to do if they are concerned that an adult they work with may lack capacity to make certain decisions.

You could make notes or your initial draft here.

FOCUS ON Commas

There are a number of places where we need to use commas. The main ones are:

- in lists
- to separate parts of sentences
- to replace brackets.

We will look at these in turn.

Commas in a list

We use commas to separate items in a list.

- For example: The fruit bowl contained apples, oranges and bananas.

A Add commas to separate items in these sentences.

1 Tuesday's lunch choices are roast pork vegetable lasagne or poached fish.

2 Moving and positioning activities include moving clients assisting in treatment and helping with daily activities such as bathing.

3 Dementia can be caused by Alzheimer's disease vascular dementia frontotemporal dementia and dementia with Lewy bodies.

4 People should see a doctor if they notice changes in their memory general mental functioning personality or ability to carry out daily tasks.

Separating parts of sentences

We also use a comma to separate two parts of a sentence. Often the comma marks off introductory words.

- For example: Despite the rain, we still enjoyed our trip to the park.

Sometimes the comma and a linking word such as 'but' or 'although' joins two possible sentences together.

- For example: Most people with dementia are over 65, but over 15,000 younger people also have dementia.

B Add commas to separate the two parts of these sentences.

1 At the age of 85 Martha still has an excellent memory.

2 In health and social care moving and positioning account for 40 per cent of work-related sickness absence.

3 To reduce moving and positioning risks carry out a proper risk assessment.

4 Following patients' suggestions mealtimes were protected and made more of an event.

Commas instead of brackets

In this case two commas mark off part of a sentence.

- For example: David Lawton, care home manager, can give you more details.

 C Add two commas to each of these sentences.

1 Mencap the learning disabilities charity has its head office in London.

2 Lisa Ross chief executive said this would never happen again.

3 Mencap describes dyslexia as a 'learning difficulty' because unlike learning disability it does not affect intellect.

4 One part of the brain called the 'hippocampus' is like a sorting centre where new sensations are compared with previous ones.

Getting a feel for commas

If you are not sure about whether to use a comma, try reading the sentence aloud. If you feel you need to pause, you may need a comma (as in this sentence).

D Read this passage out loud and decide where best to put commas.

Jane's advocate uses pictures symbols and Makaton to find out the things that are important to Jane and asks people who know Jane what they think she likes. She then supports Jane to show their work to her care manager and discuss Jane's needs and preferences. When the care manager has found some suitable places Jane and her advocate visit the homes together.

E Write out three sentences here. Then read them aloud. Do you need to use commas?

1

2

3

Managing time

Time on your hands

Managing time is important for both your work and your studies. It helps you to get the right balance between your work and personal life.

In health and social care there is always too much to do and not enough time to do it in. You need to balance the needs of different clients and make sure you give each person enough care and attention. You need to cope with unexpected crises. And you need to keep on top of records, care plans and other paperwork.

The starting point for managing your time is having clear priorities. What are the things that really matter? It is easy to spend too much time on the urgent things that keep cropping up every day and to lose sight of the more important jobs. So make sure you know what is most important. It can help to talk to your supervisor or tutor about this.

One helpful way of keeping yourself organised is to make a list of the things you need to do in the day. This gives you a clear idea of how much you need to do and how much time you can allow for each task. It is also satisfying when you start ticking off the jobs you have finished.

If you have a big task to do, such as an assignment, try breaking it down into smaller tasks. According to the saying, the way to eat an elephant is one bite at a time!

Managing time does not always mean doing things quickly. It is always worth taking the time to do a job well. This can save time in the end as you do not waste time having to do something again because you rushed it the first time.

At the same time, make sure you have breaks during the day. If you have a lunch break and, ideally, get out for some fresh air or exercise, you will come back fresher and with more energy.

A Which of these statements are true and which are false, according to the text?

1 It is important to be clear about your priorities.   True ☐   False ☐

2 Unexpected crises help you to manage time.   True ☐   False ☐

3 It is easy to spend too much time on urgent things.   True ☐   False ☐

4 It is a good idea to work through your lunch break.   True ☐   False ☐

5 It is always worth taking the time to do a job well.   True ☐   False ☐

B Write down answers to these questions.

1 Why is time management important?

2 What is the starting point for time management?

3 What is a helpful way of keeping organised?

4 Give two ways in which a to-do list can help.

a)

b)

5 What is it good to do in your lunch break?

C   In a group, discuss your own time management.

Below are some of the things that can make it harder to manage your time.

1   Which are true for you?

2   Which are true for other people?

3   Who has good ideas to avoid these problems?

Which of these things do you do?	Often	Sometimes	Never
Leave things until the last minute			
Forget to do important things			
Find it hard to say 'No'			
Spend time on things that do not matter			
Spend too much time on the phone			
Spend too much time on Facebook			
Get distracted easily			

D   Fill in the gaps in this paragraph using these words:

list   break   important   organised   distracted   priority   smaller

It is important to know which of your tasks are top [   ]. Find time

for the things that are [   ] but not urgent. If you keep a to-do

[   ], this will help you to stay [   ]. Make sure you

take a [   ] during the day as this will help you to stay fresh. Avoid

getting [   ] by things that are not important. Break up big jobs into

[   ] tasks as this can make them more manageable.

E Work with a partner. Discuss three ways in which you could manage time better. You could make notes here.

1

2

3

F Write a to-do list below.

1 Make a list here of things you need to do this week.

2 Which are the most important?

Teamwork

Teamwork and partnership working are very important in health and social care. This is because a range of people with different roles and skills may need to work together to meet all of an individual's needs.

A definition of a team is:

> **People working together to achieve a common goal or mission. Their work is interdependent and team members share responsibility for achieving the results.**

You will work in a team with your colleagues and you may work in partnership with other health and social care professionals, such as physiotherapists and occupational therapists.

The key principles of effective teamwork are:

- having shared or common goals
- openness and honesty
- trust and respect
- reliability and commitment.

Effective teams

Here are four characteristics of effective teams – and what can happen if they are not in place.

An effective team has:

- a strong sense of purpose and shared goals
- clear roles and responsibilities
- clear procedures that everyone understands
- good relationships between team members.

If this is not in place:

- there will be reduced effort and low energy
- there is less accountability and more conflict
- more time and effort will be needed to achieve tasks
- it will result in tension and stress and there will be less focus on the goals and tasks.

Communication

Good communication is essential to the smooth running of teams. It provides the basis for positive interpersonal relationships and ensures that goals and procedures are clear. There are two ways in which team members or partnership workers communicate with each other:

- Orally, by speaking and listening. In spoken communication, tone of voice and body language are as important as what we actually say.
- In writing, through instructions, notes and emails. Written communication needs to be clear so that the message cannot be misunderstood.

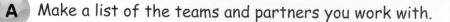

A Make a list of the teams and partners you work with.

Share your list with a partner or the rest of your group.

B Read the text and answer these questions.

1 What can happen if a team does not have clear procedures?

2 Name two things that are important in oral communication.

a)

b)

3 What can cause a team to lack energy and make less effort?

4 Give an example of a healthcare professional mentioned in the text.

5 Why is good communication important in teamwork?

C When an ending, or suffix, is added to a word, sometimes the word stays the same and sometimes the final letter 'e' is removed.

• For example:

— argue, argument, arguing

— enhance, enhancement, enhancing

Add 'ment' and 'ing' to these words.

Word	+ ment	+ ing
1 achieve		
2 treat		
3 encourage		
4 require		
5 appoint		
6 amaze		

D For each of the following words, write a sentence that contains the word.

1 Reliability

2 Accountable

3 Tension

E Read the case study and answer the questions below.

Rehabilitation centre

Edward sustained a head injury after being involved in a car crash. This resulted in brain damage that affected his mobility and speech. He was discharged from hospital to a residential rehabilitation centre. There he received care and treatment from a wide range of healthcare workers. The healthcare assistants in the centre helped him with washing, getting in and out of bed and at mealtimes. The speech therapist worked with him to regain his speech and he had physiotherapy most days to help him to walk again. The occupational therapist worked with him so that he could regain his ability to carry out daily tasks, such as getting dressed, shopping, preparing food and using public transport. The team met with the consultant every week to review Edward's progress and agree on the next steps. When he left the centre three months later he was able to walk and live independently.

1 What caused Edward's brain damage?

2 What impairments resulted from the brain damage?

3 How did the physiotherapist help Edward?

4 Who helped Edward at meal times?

5 What example of good teamwork is in the case study?

F Write a short note describing what the team you work in does that makes it effective.

FOCUS ON Questions

It may seem obvious what a question is, but people are often not sure when a question mark is needed.

A question is a statement that asks for information.

A Look at the dialogue below. Put either a question mark or a full stop at the end of each line.

David is 21 and has learning disabilities. He is at the day centre he attends two days a week. He is talking with Hilary, one of the staff.

Hilary: Hello David. How are you today

David: I'm OK, went to the park yesterday

Hilary: Oh, wasn't it a lovely day yesterday

David: It was fun

Hilary: So, what would you like to do today

David: Can I help in the kitchen

Hilary: I'm sure we can arrange that

David: What's for lunch today

Hilary: It's roast chicken and apple crumble

David: That's my favourite

B Some things sound like questions, usually because of the tone of voice in which they are said.

• For example: 'Isn't she helpful.'

This is a statement, rather than a question.

Look at the dialogue above to see if there are any statements like that.

Question words

Some words are used regularly at the start of a question, such as 'why', 'when', 'who', 'how', 'where', 'what'.

C Insert a word at the start of these statements to make a question.

1 ( ) is your favourite food?

2 ( ) is your appointment with the doctor?

3 ( ) do you live?

4 ( ) time do you need to catch the bus?

5 ( ) does she manage to do so much?

Asking questions

As a health and social care worker you will need to ask a lot of questions! You will often have to be careful about how you phrase them.

For example, if someone needs to move to another chair, you could ask: 'Can you sit somewhere else?'

But it is more polite to say: 'Would you mind moving to another chair?'

Or 'Could you sit somewhere else, please?'

Wording your question in this way is more polite and sounds more like a request than a demand or instruction.

 D Try wording these requests more tactfully.

1	What do you want to drink?	
2	Will you put that down? You will break it.	
3	Give me the report from last week's meeting.	

Open and closed questions

There are two types of questions: 'open' and 'closed' questions.

Closed questions often invite 'yes' or 'no' or very brief answers. They do not open up a conversation.

- For example: 'Do you like the new menu?'

An open question allows someone to give you more information or tell you how they think and feel.

- For example: 'What do you think of the new menu?'

 E Rewrite these closed questions as open questions.

1 Did your meeting go well?

2 Do you like the new health centre?

3 Have you had a good day?

This does not mean you should not use closed questions. They are useful for finding out precise facts or checking details.

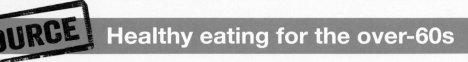

A healthy, balanced diet

Your body changes as you get older, but a balanced diet will help you to stay healthy. As you get older, you should eat:

- plenty of fruit and vegetables – aim for at least five portions of fruit and veg a day
- plenty of bread, rice, potatoes, pasta and other starchy foods – choose wholegrain varieties if you can
- some milk and dairy foods – preferably reduced fat
- some meat, fish, eggs, beans and other non-dairy sources of protein – try to eat at least two portions of fish a week, including a portion of oily fish
- just a small amount of foods and drinks that are high in fat or sugar.

Eat foods rich in fibre

Fibre-rich foods can prevent constipation and other digestive disorders. They include wholegrain or brown bread, rice, pasta and breakfast cereals, as well as potatoes, oats, beans, peas, lentils, fruit and vegetables.

Eat foods rich in iron

Iron is important for our general health. It is found in lean red meat, pulses (such as peas, beans and lentils), oily fish (such as sardines), eggs, bread, green vegetables and breakfast cereals with added vitamins.

Eat foods rich in calcium

Osteoporosis a major health issue for older people, particularly women. It develops when your bone density reduces, which increases your risk of fractures. Calcium can help you to avoid osteoporosis. Calcium is found in dairy products such as milk, cheese and yoghurt, canned fish with bones such as sardines, green leafy vegetables such as broccoli and cabbage (but not spinach), soya beans and tofu.

Eat less salt

Too much salt can raise your blood pressure, which increases the risk of health problems such as heart disease or stroke. Try to have less than 6 g of salt a day. Ready-prepared foods such as cereals, bread and tinned soups are often high in salt – read the labels.

Enough vitamin D

Vitamin D is also essential for healthy bones as it helps you absorb calcium. We mainly get our vitamin D through sunshine. Dietary sources include eggs, oily fish and some fortified breakfast cereals and spreads.

Avoid too much vitamin A

Eating more than 1.5 mg of vitamin A each day might increase your risk of bone fracture. Foods with a lot of vitamin A include liver and fish liver oils.

A Write down answers to these questions.

1 Who do you think the text is written for?

2 What is its purpose?

3 Do you think the information in it is trustworthy?

B True or false?

Which of these statements is true or false, according to the text?

1 Fibre can help to prevent digestive disorders.   True ☐   False ☐

2 White bread, rice and pasta are high in fibre.   True ☐   False ☐

3 Vitamin A can reduce the risk of bone fracture.   True ☐   False ☐

4 Eat at least five portions of fruit and veg a day.   True ☐   False ☐

5 Bone density decreases with osteoporosis.   True ☐   False ☐

6 It is OK to eat 10g of salt a day.   True ☐   False ☐

C Match these foods to what they contain.

Food		Contains	
1	Milk	a)	Iron
2	Liver	b)	Calcium
3	Sardines	c)	Salt
4	Eggs	d)	Vitamin A
5	Tinned soups	e)	Vitamin D

D A person over 60 asks you these questions. With a partner, practise replying to them.

1   I am worried about osteoporosis. What can I eat to reduce the risk?

2   My doctor has told me to eat less salt. How can I do this?

3   How can I increase the fibre in my diet?

4   Why is vitamin D important?

E Read the text again and identify the main points it contains.

You can do this in several ways. For example, you can:

- use a highlighter pen or underline key phrases or sentences
- cross out sentences (or paragraphs) that you do not need
- make notes here of the key words and phrases.

F Draft a 100-word summary of the text that you could give to a person over 60 who would like brief guidance on what they should eat.

The original text is nearly 400 words long and your task is to cut it down to around 100 words.

1 In the space below or on a separate piece of paper, make notes of the main points.

2 Read the text again to check that you have included all of the main points.

3 Write up your summary, using your notes rather than the original text – this will help you to use your own words where possible.

G Check what you have written.

- Is the length right (around 100 words)?

- Have you included all of your main points?

- Is the summary clear and concise?

- Is the punctuation and spelling OK?

Make any changes that you wish to make.

A lot of Heart n Soul

Heart n Soul is a leading creative arts company with learning disability culture at its heart. It was formed in 1986 by Mark Williams and Pino Frumiento, a musician with learning disabilities, and named after a song with that title, written by Pino.

At Heart n Soul diverse artists and participants work together towards their goal of making a more creative, fun and open world.

Heart n Soul offers a range of opportunities for people to take part, train in a new skill, or develop their artistic talents. Artists and participants share their work live, recorded or online for as many different people to enjoy as possible.

People with a learning disability are involved in real roles in every part of Heart n Soul. The organisation believes that people are capable of more, and use this as the starting point for all engagement.

They reach over 30,000 people per year in live events, creative sessions and online. This is growing every year.

Projects and events

Pioneering a multimedia club night, The Beautiful Octopus Club showcases music, theatre and dance from artists with learning disabilities. The club is aimed at adults over 18.

The Squidz Club is a participatory arts club night run 2–3 times a year that encourages young people to take part in DJing, VJing and performing arts. The club is for young people with learning disabilities (aged 10–25 years), their families and friends.

Do Your Own Thing offers creative training sessions that happen once a month on Saturday afternoons. It offers training in music, dance, drama or digital arts for young people who are new to the arts.

The Dean Rodney Singers is Heart n Soul's most ambitious project. Led by autistic artist Dean Rodney, it aims to bring to life Dean's fantasy world of mysterious creatures and superheroes that live in a parallel universe.

Dean has done this by working with 72 band members, made up of musicians, singers and dancers from seven countries across the world. Twenty-three songs and dance videos have been created using iPad apps. Each country has worked on three to four songs and band members have used iPads with cutting-edge web technology to create their own remixes and new dance videos. It has been commissioned by Unlimited, a project celebrating disability, arts, culture and sport as part of the London 2012 Cultural Olympiad.

A For each of the following words, write a sentence that contains the word.

1 Participants

2 Diverse

3 Capable

B Read the text and answer these questions.

1 Which club is aimed at young people aged 18 and above?

2 Where did the name 'Heart n Soul' come from?

3 What happens at the 'Do Your Own Thing' sessions?

4 What learning disability does Dean Rodney have?

5 What is Dean's fantasy world?

C Choose one of the words from the list below to fill the gaps in the quote from Mark Williams.

talk   segregated   chosen   society   disadvantage   prejudice   level

There's a huge mountain to climb for people with learning disabilities getting

the same [＿＿＿＿＿＿＿＿＿] of opportunity. People have to fight against

the [＿＿＿＿＿＿＿＿＿] they face because of the way they may look or

[＿＿＿＿＿＿＿＿＿]. For many years it's been a case that they've been effectively

[＿＿＿＿＿＿＿＿＿] by the way that [＿＿＿＿＿＿＿＿＿] has [＿＿＿＿＿＿＿＿＿] to

involve them in life and so there's a huge [＿＿＿＿＿＿＿＿＿] by not being included.

D The text about Heart n Soul on page 59 is about 400 words long. Write a summary of it of between 100 and 150 words.

E Read the case study and answer the questions below.

What is a VJ?

VJ stands for video jockey. VJing is the manipulation or selection of visuals, the same way DJing is a selection and manipulation of audio.

VJing often takes place at events such as concerts, nightclubs and music festivals. It is sometimes done in combination with other performing arts, resulting in a live multimedia performance that can include music, actors and dancers.

Characteristics of VJing are the technological creation or manipulation of imagery in real time for an audience, in synchronisation to music. One of the key elements of VJing is the real-time mix of content from a library of media, on DVD, video and still image files stored on computer hard drives. Content can also come from live camera input or from computer-generated visuals.

Discuss VJing in your group.

- How many of you know what it is?

- Has anyone seen a VJ performance?

- Heart n Soul helps young people with learning disabilities to learn how to do VJing. How could this art form provide an important creative opportunity for them?

F Answer these questions.

1 Where might you see a VJ?

2 What is meant by the phrase 'real-time mix of content'?

3 Who might be involved in the live performance with the VJ?

4 Give two examples of the media that could be used by a VJ.

5 Where would a DJ store their media library?

FOCUS ON Audience and purpose

Whenever you say or write anything, you need to be clear about:

- who you are speaking or writing to – your audience
- why you are speaking or writing – your purpose.

This is especially important when you are planning a letter, report, talk or presentation.

Your audience

Things to think about for your audience include:

- who they are and whether you know them already
- why they will read or listen to what you write or say
- what is likely to interest them
- which style is likely to be appropriate or inappropriate
- how much they know about the subject
- whether they will know technical terms
- whether they may have any difficulty listening or reading.

A Who might be the audience for each of these items?

Possible audiences are tutor, manager, fellow students, work colleagues, or friends.

1 Assignment for your course.

2 Text saying where to meet tonight.

3 Talk about a work placement.

4 Report about equipment to help with moving clients.

B Imagine you are writing an assignment for your tutor, which of these statements are true and which are false?

1 You should use a formal style.   True ☐   False ☐

2 You should make it amusing.   True ☐   False ☐

3 You should have a clear structure.   True ☐   False ☐

4 You should not include technical terms.   True ☐   False ☐

5 You should stick to the topic.   True ☐   False ☐

C Who is the audience, and what is the purpose of this text?

Contact dermatitis is the most common form of work-related skin disease suffered by health and social care workers. Each year an estimated 1,000 nurses develop work-related contact dermatitis. Dermatitis is an inflammatory condition of the skin caused by contact with outside agents which can result in irritation, redness, cracking and blistering. Following three simple steps can prevent dermatitis: avoid contact with materials that cause dermatitis; protect the skin; check for early signs of dermatitis.

D Who is the audience, and what is the purpose of this text?

Ministers stepped in after police arrested four people following a BBC *Panorama* documentary showing the 'inhumane abuse' of adults with learning disabilities and autism. Winterbourne View in Bristol is funded by the taxpayer and costs £3,500 a week. Undercover filming showed patients at the home being pinned down, slapped, doused in cold water and repeatedly taunted and teased.

Health and social care work depends on good communication skills. You need to be able to communicate well with clients and their families, but it is also vital to communicate well with your colleagues (the other people you work with).

An important part of being a good communicator is being sensitive to other people. This can involve three key things:

- Respect – which means showing other people that you care about them or value their views by behaving in a respectful way.
- Empathy – which means trying to understand another person's feelings as if they were your own – 'putting yourself in their shoes'.
- Trust – which means showing other people that they can count on you to do what you say you will do and to support them.

Give and take

Good communication with colleagues also depends on good information sharing.

- Giving information – you may need to pass on information to someone replacing you at the end of your shift. You may need to report something to your manager or you may need to give a client a message. In all of these cases you need to remember to share the information promptly, clearly and accurately.
- Listening carefully to what other people say – you will also receive information from colleagues. You need to listen to what they say and check if you do not understand something.

Bear in mind that several things can also get in the way of sharing information. Barriers to communication can result from:

- the way the message is communicated (e.g. using ambiguous words or phrases, using complex technical terms, mumbling or writing badly)
- the way the message is received (e.g. the person listening or reading may be tired, hard of hearing or may not understand the language used)
- the environment (e.g. a noisy room, interruptions from other people, an email not getting through or a crackly mobile phone line).

Good communication also depends on being prepared to ask for help, advice and support when you need it, and being prepared to accept offers of help from colleagues. In turn, you should be prepared and ready to offer help, advice and support when this is appropriate.

A Match these terms to their definitions.

Terms	Definitions
1 Respect	a) showing other people that they can count on you
2 Empathy	b) showing other people that you care about them or value their views
3 Trust	c) trying to understand another person's feelings as if they were your own

B Write down answers to these questions.

1 Which two groups of people must a care worker communicate with?

2 In the text, what three examples were provided of when you need to give information?

a)

b)

c)

3 List the three barriers to communication that were provided in the text.

a)

b)

c)

C In your group, read this text.

People may not contribute fully to a discussion because they are shy or lack confidence; they may feel they do not know enough about a topic to contribute; or they may be put off because other people dominate the discussion. You can find ways of encouraging them to say things without them feeling threatened.

In your group, discuss:

- things you can do before a discussion to help people participate
- things you can do during the discussion to help everyone feel involved
- things that might discourage people from participating that you should avoid during discussions.

D Reflect on how well the discussion went.

Look at these pairs of statements and decide in each case whether statement A or B was more true of your group discussion.

Statement A					Statement B
The discussion had a clear focus.	4	3	2	1	The purpose of the discussion was vague.
Everybody participated.	4	3	2	1	One or two people talked most of the time.
The discussion was lively and interesting.	4	3	2	1	The discussion was dull and boring.
The discussion stayed focused on the point.	4	3	2	1	The discussion often wandered off the point.
The discussion moved on from one topic to the next.	4	3	2	1	The discussion got bogged down in one topic.
We covered all of the discussion points.	4	3	2	1	We only covered one or two discussion points.
We ended on time.	4	3	2	1	We went well over time.

E Read this text with a partner.

Ground rules

Formal discussions need certain rules if they are to work well. Ground rules set out the behaviours that are or are not acceptable in the group. They can include:

- practical rules (e.g. we arrive on time)
- rules about how we work (e.g. we only have one conversation at a time)
- rules about how we interact (e.g. we listen to what each other says).

Ground rules help a group to operate effectively and to create a positive and constructive atmosphere. If everyone takes part in agreeing the ground rules, they are more likely to follow them than if one person imposes them.

Identify two ways you could have helped your discussion to go better.

1

2

F Use this checklist to help you move discussions forward.

Discussions can get bogged down, and you can find yourself spending too much time on one issue and then having to rush through other important topics. Here are some techniques for helping to move a discussion forward.

☐ Give a short summary of what has been said.

☐ Remind the group about the time that is available.

☐ If contributions are not relevant, gently remind people of the topic.

☐ If two or three people are dominating the discussion, invite other people to contribute who have not yet done so.

☐ If you get bogged down on a topic, consider asking one or two people to take this forward after the meeting.

☐ Try to draw a topic to an end by saying, for example, 'It sounds as if we have agreed that ...'.

☐ Encourage the group to move on by saying, for example, 'Should we move on to the next topic now?'

G Write a message.

At times you may need to leave a written message for a colleague or your manager.

> Mr S has had a sleepless night and has been feeling tired all morning. He has decided that he wants to try to sleep for an hour or so during the afternoon but would like to be woken up half an hour before teatime. Your shift finishes while he is asleep and you need to leave a message for the person replacing you.

Write your message here.

What is a hearing aid?

A hearing aid is simply a device that receives a sound and then converts and amplifies it so that the user can understand it better.

This is done digitally by altering the volume of certain tones (frequencies) to match it to the person's hearing loss. All digital instruments contain a tiny programmable chip that allows the hearing care professional to adjust and match the instrument to the user's hearing loss, which was recorded during a hearing test.

There are a number of different ranges of hearing aid technologies and styles. Which one is selected depends on the individual's preference, lifestyle and budget.

The hearing care professional will be able to talk through all of the available options and give independent advice as to which product they feel will be most suitable.

Custom hearing aids

Custom hearing aids are bespoke. They are moulded for your ear canal for maximum performance and comfort. Available in a range of skin colours, they are inconspicuous yet effective for mild to severe hearing loss.

Micro-in-the-canal (MIC) models offer the smallest possible custom solutions and are crafted to fit entirely in your ear canal using computer-aided design and the latest generation of advanced materials.

Completely-in-the-canal (CIC) models are rarely visible and cosmetically appealing. These tiny hearing aids are most suitable for mild to moderate hearing losses.

In-the-canal (ITC) models are small custom-made hearing aids that are partially visible in the outer ear yet still highly inconspicuous and have wireless functionalities.

Behind-the-ear (BTE) models

In a BTE model, the case generally sits behind the earlobe with the connection from the case coming down the front and into the ear. BTE hearing aids can address most types of hearing loss, from mild to profound. BTE aids are commonly worn by children who need a durable type of hearing aid.

BTE models are available in a variety of colours that can even blend with skin and hair colours.

BTE hearing instruments that place the loudspeaker directly in the ear without a fitted earmould are often referred to as 'receiver in the canal' instruments.

Micro CRT (canal receiver technology) hearing aids are stylish and virtually unnoticeable when worn behind the ear. The unique design allows the receiver to be separated from the hearing aid and instead sit in the ear canal. This results in some of the smallest behind-the-ear hearing aids in the world.

A Write down what the following words and phrases mean.

1	Amplifies	
2	Bespoke	
3	Cosmetically appealing	
4	Partially visible	
5	Inconspicuous	

B Use your understanding of the text to fill in the missing words.

1 Custom hearing aids are _____ to fit your ear canal.

2 Micro-in-the-canal models offer the _____ possible custom solution.

3 The hearing-aid professional will give you _____ advice.

4 A hearing aid receives a sound and converts and _____ it.

5 BTE hearing aids are commonly worn by _____. CIC hearing aids are rarely _____.

6 Micro CRT hearing aids separate the _____ from the hearing aid.

7 A hearing _____ is used to match the aid to the user's hearing loss.

C Reread the text about hearing aids and answer the questions below.

1 Which hearing aid is suitable for mild to moderate hearing loss?

2 What might influence an individual's choice of hearing aid?

3 What is the main difference between a custom hearing aid and a BTE hearing aid?

4 What does CRT stand for?

D Read the two adverts. Are the statements below true or false?

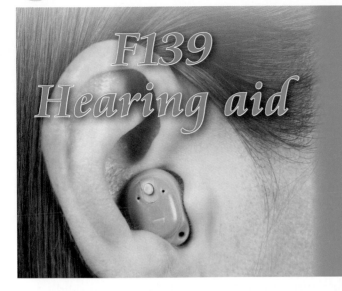

F139 Hearing aid

Product features

- Small F139 hearing aid

- Increases hearing power instantly!

- Suitable for all ages

- Ideal for partially deaf & hard of hearing

- Comfortable fit & almost invisible!

HD100 Digital micro hearing aid

Product features

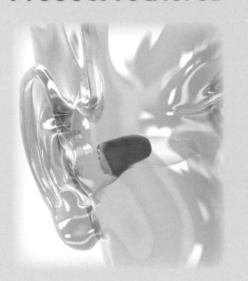

Specifically designed for high tone and age-related hearing loss

Pre-programmed with focus on speech tones

Price includes a free packet of batteries

Discreet invisible design

Digital sound technology

1 The F139 hearing aid uses digital technology. True ☐ False ☐

2 The HD100 hearing aid is good for age-related hearing loss. True ☐ False ☐

3 The F139 would be appropriate for a child. True ☐ False ☐

4 You get free batteries with the F139. True ☐ False ☐

5 The HD100 would be good for someone who does not want people to know that they wear a hearing aid. True ☐ False ☐

E Look at the adverts again.

What techniques and language is used to persuade people to buy each product?

1   F139 hearing aid

2   HD100 hearing aid

F A lot of people are reluctant to wear hearing aids, even though they have hearing loss.

Discuss with a partner what the reasons for this could be.

Make a note of all the reasons your group suggested.

FOCUS ON Checking written work

Checking what you have written is really important. It is not just people who struggle with spelling who need to check their work. We all make mistakes without meaning to, especially when using a word processor.

Think about publishers – they employ proofreaders to check books before they are printed even though they have been written by professional writers.

A Read these tips about how to proofread your work. Look out for mistakes, or 'typos', and underline the ones you find.

Proofreading tips

Profreading is the task of reading and correcting wirtten work. Its best to proofread a paper copy, rather than checking on screen as you will spot erors more easily.

You need to concentrate to do proof reading. Find a quite space where you will not distracted. First, scan your document to make sure the layout is clear Mark anything that looks odd and check pargraphs and headings.

When checking n detail you might put a ruler or peice of paper below the line you are reading to help you focus? Each sentence should start with a capital leter and end with appropriate punctutation such as a fullstop or question mark:

All words must be spelt correct. You can use a dictionery or spellchecker, but you need to be careful with spell checkers as they wont always pick up the right word for the meaning. They will miss spellinh mistakes when a typing error has changed one word ibnto another perfectly good one, such as learner/leaner, where/were, to/too.

B Write the correct spelling of any words that were misspelt.

Which documents need to be checked?

You should check everything you write. Just one missing word in an email to a friend can completely change the meaning or cause confusion, for example if you are making an arrangement to meet. But not everything needs to be perfect.

C Tick the documents below that you think need to be thoroughly checked.

☐ A note to your mum saying you have gone out and when you will be back

☐ An email applying for a job

☐ An assignment for your course

☐ An email to a friend

Proofreading checklist

Use this checklist when you proofread an important document.

☐ Scan the whole document – is the layout neat and clear?

☐ Look at the paragraphs – they do not all have to be the same length but are there any that are very long or very short?

☐ Are your headings clear with consistent use of fonts and spacing?

☐ Is the order logical and do the headings help to sequence the content?

☐ Check the titles, captions and position of any tables or illustrations.

☐ Read every sentence and word to look for errors.

☐ Make sure every sentence makes sense and conveys a complete idea.

☐ If you make a correction, read through the whole sentence again to check that it makes sense.

☐ Check sentence punctuation. Do all sentences begin with a capital letter and end with a full stop, question mark or exclamation mark?

☐ Check you have spelt any proper names correctly and used capital letters where they are needed.

☐ If you have used quotations in inverted commas, make sure you have used either single (') or double (") inverted commas consistently.

☐ Check that references at the end of the document are complete and use the required form.

Ask a friend

It is a good idea to ask someone else to proofread your work. This is because when we check our own work we see what we meant to write rather than what we have actually written. Someone else may spot errors that we miss.

And checking someone else's work will help you to recognise problems and avoid them yourself in the future.

SUCCEEDING IN INTERVIEWS

You should see any sort of job interview as a two-way exchange of information. The interviewer is trying to find out some important things about you – your skills, attitudes, experience and interests – to help them decide whether you are the right person for the job. At the same time you want to find out more about the organisation or company so that you can work out if this is the right job for you.

FIRST IMPRESSIONS REALLY COUNT

It is a sad fact that people form an opinion of someone in the first 10 seconds or so of meeting them. In an interview, that can make a big difference to your chances of getting the job. It can be very difficult to recover from a bad first impression. Below is a breakdown of the importance of three key factors in making a good impression, based on research.

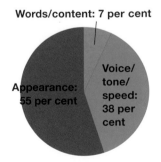

Words/content: 7 per cent

Voice/ tone/ speed: 38 per cent

Appearance: 55 per cent

In other words, *how* you look and the *way* that you talk are more important than *what* you say!

One aspect of appearance is your body language – how you walk and stand, your gestures and facial expression. Even the interviewer may not be aware that they are responding to this.

USE BODY LANGUAGE WELL

- Smile at the beginning of the interview and look at the interviewer.
- Offer a firm handshake.
- Sit back into your seat. This can help you to look and feel more confident.
- Do not cross your arms – folded arms can make you appear unfriendly and defensive and can be a barrier to communication.
- Maintain regular eye contact with the interviewer but do not stare at them.
- Respond to the interviewer with gestures such as nods and turn towards them to show that you are listening.

THE WAY THAT YOU LOOK

If you search the internet for tips on how to dress for an interview you will find that quite a few sites recommend formal dress – smart suit/dress, tie, etc. But in some sectors, formal clothes may not be appropriate, so the best advice is to choose the most *suitable* clothing. Here are a few tips in terms of appearance:

- Wear clothes in which you feel comfortable and confident.
- Make sure that your clothes are clean and tidy, including your shoes.
- Make sure that you have a bath or shower on the morning of your interview.
- Make sure that you look well groomed. This means neat hair, clean nails and face, etc.
- Do not wear revealing clothes, anything too wacky, too much make-up or jewellery.
- Do not smoke just before an interview – if you feel you must smoke, use a breath freshener.

A Read the text and choose the correct answer.

1 What is the most important factor in making a good impression?

a) Your tone of voice ☐

b) What you say ☐

c) Your appearance ☐

2 Which of the following is a form of body language?

a) Smiling ☐

b) Wearing revealing clothes ☐

c) Smoking ☐

3 How long does it usually take someone to form an opinion of you?

a) Approximately a minute ☐

b) About 10 seconds ☐

c) Five minutes ☐

4 How should you dress for an interview?

a) You should always wear a jacket or suit ☐

b) You should choose suitable clothing ☐

c) You should wear clothes that will grab the interviewer's attention ☐

5 What advice is given about eye contact?

a) Look the interviewer in the eyes as often as possible ☐

b) Do not look the interviewer in the eyes – it is bad manners ☐

c) Make regular eye contact but do not stare ☐

B What are the main 'selling points' you can offer a potential employer?

• What jobs or work experience have you had?

• What skills and qualifications do you have?

• What equipment can you use?

• What aspects of your personality or attitudes make you a good employee?

C   Think of a job you would like to do.

If you got a job interview tomorrow, what would you wear?

Share your answer with a partner.

 D   Write a short description of a job you would like to do. It should include:

- the job title
- the organisation or company
- what the job involves
- what skills they are looking for
- what sort of person they are looking for.

E   Using the job description you have written, think about how you would answer the following questions in an interview for a job or a work experience placement.

1   What interests you about this job or place of work?

2   How would this job/placement help you with your course or future career?

3   Why are you suitable for this job/placement?

F What you say in an interview matters, but listening effectively can be just as important.

1 Why do you think that listening in an interview is important?

2 How can you use body language to show that you are listening?

G Work in groups of three. Decide on a job that you could all do or choose one of the job descriptions from exercise D.

Take it in turns to interview each other for the job, with one person acting as interviewer, one as interviewee and one observing. The observer will complete the checklist below.

Start the interview by walking into the room and sitting down. The interviews only need to be about five minutes long.

First impressions				Manners
Excellent		5		Charming
Good		4		Agreeable
Satisfactory		3		Satisfactory
Not very good		2		Awkward
Unfavourable		1		Offensive
Oral communication				**Body language**
Excellent choice of words		5		Very effective
Good choice of words		4		Good, positive
Sometimes lost for words		3		Limited, neutral
Limited vocabulary		2		Poor, would not impress
Poor		1		Would create a negative effect

Tips for talking

☐ As with appearance, the important thing is to come across as comfortable and natural.

☐ Use correct grammar.

☐ Speak clearly.

☐ Do not talk too loudly or too quietly.

☐ Try to convey enthusiasm and interest.

☐ Do not use slang or swear words.

Helping people with dementia to express themselves

Active listening often helps people with dementia to express themselves more effectively. This is particularly important if the person is experiencing difficult emotions. By using these techniques we convey our empathy, which can help the person feel safe enough to open up about what's bothering them. Furthermore, using the active listening techniques of repeating, paraphrasing, reflecting and focusing also gives the person an opportunity to hear what they have communicated and clarify or expand on it. Importantly, when we listen actively, the person with dementia is taking the lead in the interaction and we are more likely to discover what's important to them.

ESMI Weekend Day Centre in Stockport uses active listening as one of a range of approaches in its work with people with dementia. In this example, Rose and Derek are pseudonyms but the conversation is a true event.

Rose suddenly becomes tearful and agitated. She stands up from her chair and looks around, as if searching for something or someone.

I approach Rose, mirroring her sadness with my own facial expression, and say, 'Rose, you look sad.'

'Sad … yes,' she says.

I ask, 'Why are you sad?'

'Can't … not … where.'

'You can't?'

'No, can't get …' Again, Rose looks around, as if searching.

'Can't get? … Can't find?'

'Find. Yes.'

'You can't find something?'

'Yes.' Rose's eyes widen at being understood. She becomes more animated and less distressed.

'Can't find what?'

She takes my hand and leads me to a door. 'Gone there.'

'Gone outside … Do you mean Derek?'

'Derek. Derek. Yes.'

Rose relaxes and her face looks happier. I have understood what is worrying her and now I can answer her concerns by explaining where Derek is and when he will return. She frequently gets upset about her husband not being here, but we always try and work out whether this is what's concerning Rose, rather than assuming. It helps her to feel that she's being listened to and she is visibly relieved when she feels someone understands.

A Write down answers to these questions.

1 What are four techniques of active listening described in the first paragraph?

2 Give two benefits of active listening described in the first paragraph.

a)

b)

3 Are 'Rose' and 'Derek' the real names of the people involved?

4 Find an example in the dialogue where the care worker uses the skill of paraphrasing.

5 Find an example in the dialogue where the care worker uses the skill of focusing.

B Look at how the quote marks in the following sentence show what the care worker said. There is also a comma before the speech begins and a full stop at the end of what the care worker says.

I approach Rose, mirroring her sadness with my own facial expression, and say, 'Rose, you look sad.'

Punctuate the following parts of the conversation with quote marks, commas and full stops when needed.

1 Sad … yes she says.

2 I ask Why are you sad?

3 Can't … not … where

4 You can't?

5 No, can't get … Again, Rose looks around, as if searching.

C Match these terms from the text to their definitions.

Terms		Definitions	
1	Empathy	a)	narrowing something down
2	Paraphrasing	b)	reflecting
3	Focusing	c)	putting something in new words
4	Mirroring	d)	a false name
5	Pseudonym	e)	trying to understand another person's feelings

 D Act out the dialogue between Rose and the care worker.

Work with two other people.

- One person plays the care worker.
- One person plays Rose.
- One person is an observer.

Afterwards, the observer should comment on how it went.

When you have finished, swap roles.

 E With a partner, write a similar dialogue between a care worker and one of the clients you work with.

1 Write the dialogue below. Try to include some of the skills used in the text.

2 Practise acting the dialogue together.

3 You could then act it out in front of other people in your group.

F Write a short story about or description of one of the clients you work with. Aim for at least three paragraphs:

- A paragraph about the client and their background
- A paragraph about the way you support them
- A paragraph about a particularly memorable incident with this client

G Exchange your short story with a partner and check each other's work.

- Does each paragraph have one main idea?
- Is it easy to read and follow?
- Is the spelling and punctuation correct?

FOCUS ON Active listening

Some people are described as 'good listeners'. When you think about someone who is good at conversation you may find that it is because they listen more than they speak. Being able to listen attentively and remember what people say is a valuable skill.

A How do you feel if someone you are talking to does the following things?

1   Interrupts you while you are speaking

2   Spends their time leafing through some papers

3   Yawns

4   Keeps looking at their watch

These are all examples of poor listening habits – they make us feel uncomfortable and ill at ease.

B How do you feel if someone you are talking to does the following things?

1   Looks at you kindly

2   Nods their head in agreement

3   Smiles

4   Asks you appropriate questions

These are examples of good listening habits – they make us feel more comfortable and 'listened to'.

We can all become better listeners by using what is known as 'active listening'. Active listening involves really paying attention to people when they speak, being interested in what they are saying and showing that you are listening.

Active listening checklist

Use this checklist to practise active listening skills.

- ☐ Do not try to do other things when you are meant to be listening.

- ☐ Sit or stand at the same level so that you can see the other person comfortably. Make sure there is enough space to hear each other clearly without crowding them.

- ☐ Use eye contact well; look at the other person regularly without staring at them.

- ☐ Use positive body language, such as leaning forward, smiling and other facial expressions.

- ☐ Avoid things that show lack of interest or impatience, like folded arms, yawning or tapping your fingers.

- ☐ Give the speaker time to think and organise their thoughts.

- ☐ Do not interrupt.

- ☐ Nod your head. Encourage with comments like 'Yes' and 'I see'.

- ☐ Check your understanding of what the person has said from time to time. Say, 'So you mean ... ?'

- ☐ Ask questions to show interest and to encourage the other person to continue.

- ☐ Try to really *hear* what the person is trying to say. Avoid jumping to conclusions or judging people.

Practise using these techniques next time you listen to someone, whether one to one or in a group.

SOURCE | **Mental health in young people**

What is mental illness?

It is important to be sure what we mean by mental illness. Most of us cope well enough with our lives on a day-to-day basis. But there are times when we don't feel so well. We get fed up, lonely, disappointed; we become anxious or frightened. We feel misunderstood and let things get out of proportion.

These kinds of feelings are part and parcel of ordinary living. But sometimes they get on top of us – so much so that we find we can't get on with our lives. We can't concentrate and sometimes we can't get to work or school. We seem to be at odds – with other people and with ourselves. Our behaviour may get 'out of order' and we may become restless, argumentative, even violent. We are not happy. We don't feel well.

When our lives become as difficult as this, we have mental health problems. They can be mild or severe – some get better quickly but sometimes they last a long time and people need a lot of help.

The term 'mental illness' refers to the extreme end of these difficulties when some people, at different times of their lives, become so confused and out of touch with reality that they can barely cope with everyday living.

'We get fed up, lonely, disappointed; we become anxious or frightened. We feel misunderstood and let things get out of proportion.'

A What is the main purpose of the 'What is mental illness?' text?

B Who do you think the text is written for?

C Which one of these statements best defines mental illness, according to the text?

1 Feeling fed up, lonely and disappointed; becoming anxious and frightened. ☐

2 Becoming too confused and out of touch with reality to cope with everyday living. ☐

3 Feeling misunderstood and letting things get out of proportion. ☐

4 Feeling unhappy and unwell. ☐

D Using the information in the text, give two examples of what happens when feelings get on top of us.

1

2

E Give two features of the text that help to convey information.

1

2

Improving the mental health of Northern Ireland's children and young people

EXECUTIVE SUMMARY
SECTION A – INTRODUCTION
Chapter 1 – Background and scope of the review

This report is one of five rapid reviews commissioned by the Health and Social Care Research and Development Division of the Public Health Agency (PHA). It presents a series of overviews of effectiveness research relevant to the mental health of children and young people in Northern Ireland. This review covers the subgroups identified as priority areas of research by the PHA following consultation with policymakers, practitioners and commissioners, namely:

- Early Interventions
- Mental Health of Looked After Children
- Development of Resilience.

The review also covers two additional areas of importance highlighted by the Bamford report, namely:

- Children with Autism Spectrum Disorders and Complex Needs
- Gay, Lesbian, Bisexual and Transgender Youth.

The overall purpose of this report is to map the current evidence base in relation to 'what works' in each of the five identified areas, by considering the available literature, identifying policy implications, examining specific subthemes and identifying the key research questions requiring attention in future research. This executive summary highlights some of the substantive findings emerging from the review, but focuses primarily on implications for research.

F What is the main purpose of the text 'Improving the mental health of Northern Ireland's children and young people'?

G Who do you think the text is written for?

H Give two ways in which the text presents information in a different way from the earlier text 'What is mental illness?'.

1

2

I With a partner, compare the two texts. Try to find at least one strength and one weakness in each text.

J Make notes about problems with mental health in young people, drawing on the texts and your own knowledge.

Hidden dangers in health and social care

People working in health and social care are exposed to substances that could harm their health. The term for these is 'hazardous substances'. They may include chemicals, dust, fumes, microorganisms, etc.

The Control of Substances Hazardous to Health Regulations 2002 (COSHH) are there to protect workers' health in all industries. Employers have to:

- assess the risks of working with the hazardous substances
- eliminate or reduce these risks
- introduce measures to control the risks where it is not possible to eliminate them
- where necessary, monitor the health of employees.

If a COSHH risk assessment has been made, everyone has to follow it.

What are the risks?

Hazardous substances used in care homes include some cleaning materials, disinfectants and microorganisms (associated with clinical waste or soiled laundry).

Latex, which is used in many medical rubber gloves, falls under the COSHH regulations because it can cause irritation or allergic reactions in some people. So it is important for employers to have a clear policy for reducing the risks.

Drugs and medicines can be dangerous if they are not used correctly. All drugs should be labelled and stored and handled securely.

The risk assessment

To carry out COSHH risk assessments, employers must assess the health risk faced by their employees, service users and visitors, and decide on the action they need to take to prevent or control exposure to hazardous substances. They must share the results of the assessment with employees.

COSHH assessments should be relatively simple in a care home. First of all you need to establish what products and biological hazards (e.g. clinical waste or soiled laundry) are in the home. Identify if any less-harmful products can be used to reduce the risk.

If products cannot be replaced, then take precautions such as good ventilation and protective equipment. Toilet cleaners and polishes may only require the use of rubber gloves, whereas descalers and oven cleaners may require heavy-duty gloves, goggles or face shields and a well-ventilated area. Keep all cleaning materials out of the reach of vulnerable service users.

A In a group, discuss these questions.

1 Have you heard of COSHH?

2 Do you know a company that does risk assessments?

3 Who does the risk assessment?

4 What training have you had about hazardous substances?

B Match the words with their meanings.

Words		Meanings	
1	Hazardous	a)	Bacteria, virus or other small organism that may be an agent of disease
2	Latex	b)	Can harm living things or the environment
3	Eliminate	c)	Natural rubber, used to make gloves
4	Microorganism	d)	To get rid of something

C Choose two of the words above and write each of them in separate sentences.

1

2

D Write down answers to these questions.

1 Define 'hazardous substance'.

2 Why is latex defined as a hazardous substance?

3 How can you reduce the risks from medicines?

E An important part of any group discussion is responding to what other people say. If someone said the following things to you about protecting health in the workplace, what would you say?

- You cannot just reply 'I agree' or 'I disagree'.
- You need to add something more to the discussion.

1 'It takes too long to do the COSHH paperwork. I do not have the time.'

What would you say?

2 'Care workers are able to look after themselves. They do not need a nanny state telling them how to stay healthy.'

What would you say?

3 'All care homes are as bad as each other. None of them care about their workers' health and safety.'

What would you say?

4 'Care workers should take more care of their own health and safety, not leave it all to management.'

What would you say?

F With a partner, discuss a health or social care organisation that you know.

- Note down some of the hazardous substances it uses.
- How does it reduce the risks from hazardous substances?

Substance	How risk is reduced

G Draft a poster about the hidden dangers from hazardous substances for a health or social care organisation that you know. You could make some notes about what to include here.

 **FOCUS ON Quote marks**

We use quote marks (also called 'speech marks') when we want to include words that somebody has said, as in these examples.

'What time will we meet?' asked Tom.

Ruth replied, '7.30 would be good.'

Tom said, 'That's great. See you then.'

The quote marks show which words are spoken, in much the same way as speech bubbles in a cartoon.

When you should use quote marks:

- Every time a new person starts to speak, start a new paragraph.

- If you start a sentence with someone 'said' or 'replied', etc., put a comma before the quote starts.

- Put quote marks at the start and at the end of the spoken text.

- Use either single (') or double (") quote marks, but be consistent.

- Start each quote with a capital letter.

- Include punctuation (e.g. the question mark above) within the quote marks.

A Copy these sentences, but insert quote marks and other punctuation.

1 The care worker asked Are you ready for lunch yet

2 My shift starts at nine o'clock said Ed

3 When do you finish work Yusuf asked

4 Emma said May would like her tea at four

Look at the following example.

- 'That's great,' said Tom. 'See you then.'

If you have a piece of speech that is split into two parts, the punctuation is different. For example:

- There are two sets of speech marks.
- There is a comma at the end of the first piece of speech.
- There is a full stop at the end of the second piece of speech.

B Copy these sentences, but insert quote marks and other punctuation.

1 Bill has not quite eaten all his lunch said Priya He would like to go into the lounge when he is finished

2 Shall we take a wheelchair asked Jess. It might come in useful.

Inverted commas

Just as we use quote marks to show words that someone has spoken, so we can use them (or 'inverted commas') to show:

- the title of a book or article
- an extract from a book, article or the internet that you include in your writing.

You can include short extracts within a paragraph, with inverted commas before and after each title or extract.

In the article 'Helping people with dementia to express themselves' the writer argues that we can use 'active listening techniques' to 'convey our empathy' and help clients to 'feel safe enough to open up about what's bothering them'. The techniques include 'repeating, paraphrasing, reflecting and focusing' and can help clients to 'hear what they have communicated' and to take 'the lead in the interaction'.

Longer extracts may need their own paragraph.

C Try putting quote marks in this paragraph, referring back to the text on page 69.

The article What is a hearing aid? defines a hearing aid as a device that receives a sound and then converts and amplifies it so that the user can understand it better. Which hearing aid you choose depends on the individual's preference, lifestyle and budget. Examples include custom hearing aids, in-the-canal models and behind-the-ear models.

A plea for help

How can I get fresh food?

The lady below wrote to a national newspaper asking for help and advice. Here is what she wrote and some of the online replies that people posted.

At 75, with terminal cancer, I'm too tired to cook or eat out, but hate readymeals. My husband, 83, can't cook. I crave the meals I always produced from our home-grown fresh crops. Does illness and old age have to mean crap food? Any advice or ideas?

Both my grandparents and a number of people in their community use www.wiltshirefarmfoods.com to keep themselves going. **Ctoan1**

Have you got a friend who enjoys cooking? He/she might be very happy to make up a batch of home-made ready meals for you? Friends may be keen to help but not know what kind of support you need. I wish you well. **Alicecat**

I'm generally unable to cook for myself, due to health problems, and have had to resort to ready meals. Two companies who make good meals (made from real ingredients) are 'Cook' and 'Look what we found.' www.lookwhatwefound.co.uk/landing. Another possibility might be to find someone who could batch cook for your freezer, so that you had a supply of home cooked foods which just needed heating up. **SerenaB**

I love to cook and would gladly come round and help if I lived nearby. Surely there must be other people like me? Could your local Council for Voluntary Action find a willing volunteer? If anyone deserves to eat healthy, nourishing and enjoyable food, you do. **JKayC**

Next time someone says 'let me know if there's anything I can do', say 'Actually there is. You make a fab whatever, would you make me some for the freezer?' I'm guessing it will work better with meals like curry, soup, lasagne, chilli, etc. that freeze well. I'd be delighted to do the same for a friend in a similar situation. **limegreen**

Is your husband in charge of the garden, and is the fresh produce still available? If so, could you offer some of the veg to someone you know, or through Gumtree, or a card in a local shop, and ask that they bring you something made from it in return? **whood**

I'd endorse an earlier comment about Wiltshire Farm Foods – my dad uses them and they also have the great advantage of being simple to order by phone and then deliver to you so take very little effort to arrange. **Hermione**

I live in Suffolk if that's any good, and would happily help. I love cooking and grow my own stuff (though the results can be a bit hit and miss). Failing that, from the posts on here, it is clear that there are lots of people of a similar mind which leads me to think that if you wrote something in your village newsletter (or local paper) you would be deluged with offers of help. **oskarfoxtrot**

I often end up cooking more than my family can eat – you don't mention where you live. I would happily drop round some food if I am near. My thoughts are with you both. **pasteldama**

Your local branch of Age UK may run a voluntary visiting scheme – they'll do their best to match you with a vetted, CRB-checked visitor with skills and interests that meet your needs. Someone could make a once-a-week commitment to shop for you, cook the meals you enjoy and, as others have sensibly suggested, freeze it in batches for you. **intheshed**

A In your group, discuss how you felt about this problem and how you reacted to the replies.

B Reread the text and answer these questions.

1   Which three people offered to cook for this lady?

2   JkayC suggests contacting the local Council for Voluntary Action. Which other charity is suggested?

3   Give three reasons why this lady cannot get the meals she wants.

a)

b)

c)

4   Why does Alicecat suggest that friends might not have offered to help?

5   Which person also has health problems?

C Write your own post in reply to the lady's question.

D The lady says that she hates ready meals.

Why do you think this might be the case?

E Discuss ready meals with a partner.

- Do you like ready meals? Which ones have you had?
- In your opinion, which shop sells the best ready meals?
- Do you think ready meals would provide this lady with a good diet?

F Match each person with what they said.

What they said
1 find someone who could batch cook for your freezer
2 I love cooking and grow my own stuff
3 My thoughts are with you both
4 could you offer some of the veg to someone you know
5 I'd be delighted to do the same for a friend

Person
a) limegreen
b) whood
c) SerenaB
d) oskarfoxtrot
e) pasteldama

About Wiltshire Farm Foods

Wiltshire Farm Foods is the UK's leading meals delivery service

All our meals and many of our desserts in this brochure are made by us. All our meals are prepared to the very highest standards using recipes perfected by our team of chefs in Wiltshire. We take the greatest care in sourcing our ingredients and preparing our meals. Our meals are frozen the moment they are cooked and delivered across the UK & Northern Ireland through a network of local outlets.

How Wiltshire Farm Foods can help

We can offer the perfect way for you or a relative to eat well, without having to worry about long trips to the supermarket, preparing food or managing boiling pots and pans. Many of our customers have special dietary needs and so we work hard to make sure our meals and desserts meet the best nutritional standards.

❝Our meals not only look and taste great, but they're good for you too.❞

How we deliver

Wiltshire Farm Foods hand delivers our meals, free, direct to your door.

Our team of drivers normally get around to every mainland Great Britain & Northern Ireland address either weekly or fortnightly.

We know you don't want a stranger arriving at your door, which is why our drivers go through an extensive training programme, as well as a police security check, to make sure they are someone you can trust and rely on.

G Look at the text on page 95 and answer the questions.

1 Which two people recommended Wiltshire Farm Foods?

2 What two features of Wiltshire Farm Foods mean it is easy to arrange delivery of the meals?

a)

b)

3 Which two other companies are recommended and why?

H Use the information about Wiltshire Farm Foods to fill the gaps in the sentences below.

1 Wiltshire Farm Foods meals are ⬚ the moment they are cooked.

2 The meals are prepared by a team of ⬚.

3 They take great care about ⬚ their ingredients.

4 Many of their customers have special ⬚ needs.

5 Their drivers complete an extensive ⬚ programme.

I Which of these statements are true and which are false according to the text?

1	Wiltshire Farm Foods charge for delivery.	True ☐	False ☐
2	They deliver across the whole of the UK.	True ☐	False ☐
3	Their meals meet high nutritional standards.	True ☐	False ☐
4	The meals are prepared at a network of local outlets.	True ☐	False ☐
5	Drivers are checked by the police.	True ☐	False ☐
6	The meals are ready to eat when they are delivered.	True ☐	False ☐

J Write down what you think are the three top selling points for Wiltshire Farm Foods.

Share your list with your group. Then discuss these questions:

• How might they help with the lady's problem?

• What disadvantages or problems could there be?

Working time and the minimum wage

If you are under 18 but over school-leaving age you are classed as a young worker. You reach school-leaving age at the end of the summer term of the school year in which you turn 16.

Working time limits

A young worker cannot usually be made to work more than eight hours per day or 40 hours per week. These hours cannot be averaged over a longer period and you are not allowed to ignore these restrictions.

You'll only be able to work longer hours if you need to:

- keep the continuity of service or production, or
- respond to a surge in demand for a service or product.

This is provided that:

- there is no adult available to do the work, or
- your training needs are not negatively affected.

The minimum wage

You become eligible for the national minimum wage (NMW) when you're older than school-leaving age. The rate of NMW will then depend on your exact age. There isn't a national minimum wage for people under 16.

There are different levels of NMW, depending on your age and whether you are an apprentice. The rates from 1 October 2012 are:

- £6.19 per hour – the main rate for workers aged 21 and over
- £4.98 per hour – the 18–20 rate
- £3.68 per hour – the 16–17 rate for workers above school-leaving age but under 18.

The apprentice rate is £2.65 per hour for apprentices under 19, or for those aged 19 or over and in the first year of their apprenticeship.

Most workers in the UK over school-leaving age are legally entitled to be paid at least the NMW and all employers have to pay it to you if you are entitled to it. It makes no difference:

- if you are paid weekly or monthly, by cheque, in cash or in another way
- if you work full time, part time or any other working pattern
- if you work at your employer's own premises or elsewhere
- what size your employer is
- where you work in the UK.

You are entitled to the NMW even if you sign a contract agreeing to be paid at a lower rate. This is regardless of whether you sign of your own free will or because your employer persuades or makes you – you must still be paid the proper rate.

The Pay and Work Rights Helpline gives confidential help and advice on the NMW. If you need to work longer than 40 hours a week or you think your employer is unfairly asking you to work over this limit, you can call them on 0800 917 2368. The helpline can take calls in over 100 languages.

A Read the text and answer the questions.

1 What does NMW stand for?

2 What is the NMW for people aged 18–20?

3 Who can you call for help and advice about the NMW?

4 What is the maximum time each day that a young worker can be made to work for?

5 In what circumstances can a young worker be asked to exceed the working time limit?

6 When does a young person reach school-leaving age?

B Which of these statements are true and which are false according to the text?

1 The Pay and Work Rights Helpline will tell your employer that you contacted them.   True ☐   False ☐

2 A young worker cannot normally be made to work more than 40 hours a week.   True ☐   False ☐

3 The NMW does not apply to you if you are paid in cash.   True ☐   False ☐

4 An apprentice aged 25 and in their first year is entitled to a NMW of £2.65 per hour.   True ☐   False ☐

5 A young worker will be under 18 years old.   True ☐   False ☐

6 All workers above school-leaving age in the UK are entitled to a NMW of at least £4.98 per hour.   True ☐   False ☐

C Insert a word from the list below into the text so that it makes sense.

hour   jobs   minimum   increase   opposed

The national ⬭wage was introduced in the UK in 1999 when it was set
at £3.60 per ⬭. People who ⬭the NMW said that it
would reduce the number of ⬭and ⬭inflation, but
that did not happen.

D Write a sentence to answer each of the following questions. Make sure you use
capital letters and full stops where they are needed.

1 Do small employers have to pay the national minimum wage?

2 I am from Romania and my English is not very good. Will the Helpline understand me?

3 My employer made me sign a contract to be paid £2.50 an hour. Does that mean I am
not entitled to the national minimum wage?

E Read about the person below.

I am an apprentice in a care home. A lot of the other
people there work a 50- or 60-hour week. My manager
says I must do the same as it is normal in our sector and
our clients need care. I am only given the rubbish jobs
to do like clearing up and emptying the bins, I am not
learning anything. She also makes me miss my off-job
training days sometimes. It is making me really tired and
I am struggling to complete my portfolio.

What advice would you give this person?

F Discuss wages and working hours in your group.

- Do staff in health and social care work long hours?
- Do you think that workers in health and social care are well paid?
- Why do people choose to work in the health and social care?
- What do you know about trade unions? How do they help? Would you join one?

G Choose the correct answer to each of these questions.

1 The NMW for workers over 21 is:
   a) £4.98 ☐
   b) £6.19 ☐
   c) £3.68 ☐

2 The national minimum wage does not apply to:
   a) people paid a monthly salary ☐
   b) people under 16 ☐
   c) people who agree to a lower rate ☐

3 The Pay and Work Rights Helpline gives advice on:
   a) contracts of employment ☐
   b) health and safety at work ☐
   c) working time limits ☐

H Draft a leaflet for apprentices aged 16–19 telling them about their rights.

FOCUS ON Preparing a talk

You may be asked to give a talk or presentation, either as part of your course or at work. To do this well, you need to consider four key elements:

- planning
- using visual aids
- rehearsing or practising
- getting feedback.

Planning

Start by identifying a topic or subject for your presentation and then think about the purpose and audience.

- Purpose: is your presentation intended to *inform*, *persuade* or *advise*?
- Audience: What do they already know? What *language* and style is appropriate?

A presentation must have a clear structure. It should start with a general introduction telling people what the talk is about and end with a summary of what you have said.

You should then identify the main sections. For a 10-minute presentation you should have three to five main headings, organised in a logical order.

A Here are the main headings for a talk about how a heath and social care organisation handles complaints. Organise them into a logical sequence.

1 Examples of complaints

2 Summary

3 Listening to a complaint

4 Company or organisation procedures

5 Introduction

6 How complaints are resolved

Once you have identified your main headings, you can add details of what you will say under each one.

For example, under 'Listening to a complaint' your plan may include the following points:

- Be respectful and courteous.
- Find somewhere private to talk so that you can maintain confidentiality.
- Listen carefully to the individual and be aware of your body language.
- Keep calm and speak quietly to help the person relax.
- Acknowledge the complaint so that they know they have been heard.
- Do not prejudge the situation or offer your own opinion.
- Tell the person what will happen next.

B How will you plan the outline of your talk? Tick the one that suits you best.

☐ Brainstorm all of your ideas on the topic and then organise them in order.

☐ Use a mind map to organise your ideas.

☐ Write a list and then reorganise it.

☐ Use a storyboard format similar to that used for a film or video.

Using visual aids

Relevant images and visual aids can really bring a presentation to life. They can include:

- images, such as photographs, diagrams, paintings
- a model or other physical object or a wall display
- PowerPoint, whiteboard or flipchart.

If you use PowerPoint you can incorporate diagrams and pictures. Be careful not to put too many words on a slide or people will be reading it rather than listening to you.

Cue cards

Cue cards will help you when you are giving your presentation. They:

- are easy to hold and avoid long pages of notes
- remind you of your main points through key words or phrases
- will not distract your audience as much as big sheets of paper.

Here are some tips for writing cue cards:

- Use cards that are about the size of a filing card (15 cm × 10 cm).
- Write one key word or phrase for the main heading.
- Write no more than four more detailed points and number them.
- Write in large letters or capitals.
- Number your cards in case you drop them!

Practising

It is very important to practise your presentation before you do it for real. Think of it in the same way as a rehearsal for a performance. This will alert you to any gaps or areas where you may be unclear about content. It will also help you with aspects of delivery such as tone and speed of voice and language.

It's very important to practise your presentation before you do it for real. Think of it as a rehearsal for a performance. This will help both with the content and with aspects of delivery such as tone of voice and speed.

Decide whether you will practise on your own in front of a mirror or by recording yourself, with a friend, or with your tutor or in front of a small group.

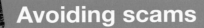

SOURCE | Avoiding scams

OFT and *Age UK* join forces to tackle scams

The Office of Fair Trading and Age UK have joined forces to raise awareness among older people of mass-marketed scams and urge them to speak up if they have been targeted by scammers.

Older people are more likely to be targeted by these scammers with over-55s accounting for almost half of the people who say they have been approached, according to OFT research.

Age UK is supporting the OFT's Scams Awareness Month as part of its Older People and Crime Initiative. This initiative involves training over 100 Age UK volunteers across England and Wales to advise on issues including scams, by visiting older people in local community groups such as at day-care centres and coffee mornings.

Helena Herklots, Services Director at Age UK, said:

'Although crime against older people is less likely than other age groups, people in later life can be an attractive target for scammers. Fortunately, a lot of scams can be avoided, provided people have the right information and advice, and know what to look out for. Age UK has produced two free information guides 'Avoiding Scams' and 'Staying Safe' which warn people of the most common scams and provide practical advice.'

Michele Shambrook, Operations Manager of Consumer Direct, commented:

'Scammers are expert at exploiting people's hopes and fears. Anyone can be conned but by learning to recognise the scammer's tricks we can all avoid becoming their next victim.

'We want older people to recognise the warning signs, and feel confident enough to seek advice from friends and family or organisations like ours.'

The OFT and Age UK are giving people the following advice:

- If you are unsure about an offer, speak to family or friends and seek advice from Consumer Direct before sending any money or giving out any banking or credit card details.

- Stop, think and be sceptical. If something sounds too good to be true, it probably is.

- Do not be rushed into sending off money to someone you do not know, however plausible they might sound and even where an approach is personalised.

- Ask yourself how likely it is that you have been especially chosen for this offer – thousands of other people will probably have received the same offer.

- Think about how much money you could lose from replying to a potential scam – it is not a gamble worth taking.

A What is the main purpose of the source 'Avoiding scams'?

[   ]

B According to the text, what proportion of people who have been approached by scammers are over 55?

1 A quarter   ☐

2 Almost half   ☐

3 Over half   ☐

4 Almost three-quarters   ☐

C According to the text, which one of these statements is true?

1 The OFT are training volunteers across England and Wales.   ☐

2 Age UK are training volunteers across the UK.   ☐

3 Scammers target day-care centres and coffee mornings.   ☐

4 Age UK volunteers advise on issues including scams.   ☐

D According to the text, identify two things to do before sending off money.

1 [   ]

2 [   ]

E Decide whether each of these statements are presented in the text as facts or opinions.

1 OFT and Age UK have joined forces to raise awareness amongst older people.
   Fact ☐   Opinion ☐

2 Scammers are expert at exploiting people's hopes and fears.
   Fact ☐   Opinion ☐

3 OFT research shows that older people are more likely to be targeted.
   Fact ☐   Opinion ☐

4 Anyone can be conned.
   Fact ☐   Opinion ☐

F Read these emails and answer the questions below.

BARCLAYS

Dear Sir/Madam,

Barclays Bank PLC. always looks forward for the high security of our clients. Some customers have been receiving an email claiming to be from Barclays advising them to follow a link to what appears to be a Barclays web site, where they are prompted to enter their personal Online Banking details. Barclays is in no way involved with this email and the web site does not belong to us.

Barclays is proud to announce about their new updated secure system. We updated our new SSL servers to give our customers a better, fast and secure online banking service.

Due to the recent update of the servers, you are requested to please update your account info at the following link.

http://www.barclays.co.uk/cgi-bin/accountupdate/1.00.102.html

J. S. Smith
Security Advisor
Barclays Bank PLC.

NatWest another way

Security Message:

Dear Value Client of NatWest,

You have received a new message from The NatWest Security Department Team about the new security update.

We urgently request that you should Sign in to read about the new security upgrade

[Read]

If you have question about your online statement, please send us an email or call us at 0846 600 2323.

Online Message Department
NatWest Online Banking

1 Who does each email claim to be from?

2 What does each email want you to do? How do they try to persuade you?

3 Should you do what the emails ask?

G Discuss scams with a partner.

- Have you ever experienced a phone or online scam?
- Do you know any older people who have suffered from a scam?
- What can be done to protect older people from scams?

H Write an email.

A member of your family (perhaps a grandparent) has received one of the scam emails. They have forwarded it to you because they are not sure what to do about it.

Write a reply to them explaining what they should do and how they can avoid being conned.

	Message	Adobe PDF								
Reply	Reply to All	Forward	Delete	Move to Folder	Create Rule	Other Actions	Block Sender	Safe Lists ▾ Not Junk	Categorize	Follow Up	Mark as Unread	Find Related ▾ Select ▾	Send to OneNote
Respond			Actions				Junk E-mail		Options		Find	OneNote

To:

Subject:

Why choose equity release?

People choose equity release for different reasons. For many people it is a natural choice to release money from their biggest asset to help fund their retirement plans. They have worked hard all their life to pay for their home. Why not benefit now?

Equity release can pay for home improvements, a new car, holidays or healthcare. Equity release can provide that extra money you are looking for to top up your income, especially if living costs increase faster than pensions and savings.

When you take a big step like releasing equity from your home, you naturally want to consult people who have a strong track record and can offer you the very best advice.

- We are one of the UK's largest providers of lifetime mortgages.
- We have been in the market for over 11 years.
- Over 113,000 people have released cash from their homes with us.
- We have helped our customers release over £3.8 billion.
- We have award-winning lifetime mortgage products.
- We have qualified advisers who can visit you in your own home or at a time and place that is convenient to you.
- We are a trusted and long-standing lifetime mortgage provider in the UK.
- We are authorised and regulated by the Financial Services Authority.
- We are a long-established member of Safe Home Income Plans (SHIP).

Many people have spent many years paying off a mortgage to build up equity in their home. And while property values are no longer racing ahead as they did, most people find their home is worth much more than they paid for it. The chart below (from the Nationwide House Price Index 2011) shows that average house prices have more than doubled over the last 20 years.

1991 £54,903

2001 £91,049

2011 £166,597

Here is what some of our customers have said:

'Equity release has given us enormous flexibility in the way we run our lives with security attached. It's made a very big difference to our lives.' Mr and Mrs Watts, Winchester

'It's been marvellous. We've never regretted it. We're more relaxed and content about everything. A happy retirement because of equity release. Brilliant.' Mr and Mrs Holmes, Barnsley

A In your group, discuss equity release.

- Have you heard of it before?
- Do you know anyone who has taken out an equity release product?
- What do you think are the advantages and disadvantages?

B What is the main purpose of the text 'Why choose equity release?'

C Decide whether each of these statements are presented in the text as facts or opinions.

1 There are many reasons why people choose equity release.   Fact ☐   Opinion ☐

2 It's made a very big difference to our lives.   Fact ☐   Opinion ☐

3 We have been in the market for over 11 years.   Fact ☐   Opinion ☐

4 We're more relaxed and content about everything.   Fact ☐   Opinion ☐

D The text is taken from a publicity brochure from an equity release provider. With a partner, circle words or phrases that are designed to persuade people to choose their equity release scheme, for example:

- 'For many people it is a natural choice to release money from their biggest asset...'
- 'We have award-winning lifetime mortgage products.'

E Write down two other techniques that the text uses to persuade readers.

1

2

F Read these comments about equity release:

Equity release is a big decision and might not be the best or only solution. Start by thinking about other ways to raise money – perhaps by moving to a smaller property or checking you're claiming all the benefits you're entitled to. Ask yourself important questions – if your circumstances change, will it affect your ability to move? If you receive benefits, what will the impact be? If you have children, how will they feel about it?

While equity release rates don't sound much higher than ordinary mortgages, they often cost much more. No repayments are made till you die, so the interest compounds rapidly. For example, borrow £20,000 aged 65 at 6.5% on a £120,000 home and live 25 years, and when you die £100,000 needs repaying. So you won't find 'best deals' on this site, as there's not one I'd be happy to suggest.

Equity release schemes are high-risk products and you should take advice before you make any decision about whether to use them. Some schemes could wipe out a huge chunk of the value of your property if you live for a long time. Often there are cheaper alternatives, such as downsizing to a smaller property. But if you don't want to move, equity release schemes can provide a way of unlocking the unused value in your home.

G Write down the benefits and disadvantages of equity release from what you have read. The list has been started for you.

Benefits	Disadvantages
It can: • top up your income	It might: • reduce the benefits you can claim

H An older person you know (it could be a member of your family) would like your advice about equity release. They are finding that their pension is only enough for day-to-day expenses and they do not have enough money for holidays or unexpected expenses like a new boiler. They have had a quote from an equity release firm to release £20,000. Their house is currently worth £120,000. They have two children and several grandchildren. You need to write to them about it.

With a partner, make a plan for what you will write. Make notes for five paragraphs as follows:

- An introductory paragraph introducing what you are writing about.

- Possible advantages of equity release schemes.

- Possible disadvantages of equity release schemes.

- Possible alternatives to equity release schemes.

- A conclusion persuading the person to think very carefully before they take up the scheme on offer.

I Produce a first draft of your five paragraphs and discuss it with your partner.

FOCUS ON Writing good paragraphs

Paragraphs are important in all pieces of writing that are more than a few sentences long. They provide a clear structure to longer emails, letters, assignments and reports. Good paragraphs divide up the text and separate out the main ideas. They make it easier for the reader to follow your argument.

The principles for writing good paragraphs are as follows:

- Use a new paragraph for each new idea.

- A paragraph can have just one or two sentences, though usually they will have three to six sentences.

- Each paragraph begins with the 'topic sentence', which introduces the idea.

- The other sentences then provide more information about this idea.

- All of the sentences should be relevant to the main idea.

Look at the first paragraph on this page. The topic sentence is the one beginning 'Paragraphs are important'. The other sentences explain why they are important. There are four sentences altogether.

A Read the following paragraph. Which is the topic sentence? How many other sentences are there?

> There are different types of paragraph. You begin your piece of writing with an introductory paragraph, which introduces what you will write and why you are writing it. You then have one paragraph for each of the main ideas. You end with a concluding paragraph, which sums up what you have said.

Punctuating paragraphs

You punctuate paragraphs like this:

- Begin a new paragraph with a new line.

- Either leave a line space before the new paragraph, or indent the first line of the paragraph.

- Each sentence begins with a capital letter and ends with a full stop (or a question mark or exclamation mark).

 B Turn the above information, about punctuating paragraphs, into a paragraph rather than a bullet list. You can use the same words, though you may want to make a few minor changes so that the paragraph reads better. Make sure you begin with a good topic sentence.

Introducing the paragraph

As we have seen, the first sentence is likely to be the topic sentence and will introduce the idea in the paragraph. Where possible, it is good to link back to what has gone before. You can do this with phrases such as 'as we have seen', 'on the other hand' or 'however'. Try to make the topic sentence as interesting as possible.

Developing the paragraph

The other sentences will develop the idea in the topic sentence. They can do this in several ways such as:

- explaining the idea in greater detail
- providing a list (like this one!)
- giving an example
- including some facts or figures.

However, the sentences must all be relevant to the topic and must never introduce a new idea.

Ending the paragraph

The final sentence may simply round off the paragraph. In some cases it may sum up what you have said or lead in to the next paragraph.

C Turn these words and phrases into a paragraph about the role of a care worker.

care worker   vital role   today's society   people of all ages

children, adults, elderly people   meal times

washing or dressing   medication   company and a chat   1.75 million UK care workers

D Next time you need to draft a paragraph, use this checklist to check what you have written.

Does the paragraph start a new line? ☐

Is there a clear topic sentence? ☐

Do other sentences develop the main idea? ☐

Are all sentences relevant to the main idea? ☐

Is the paragraph interesting? ☐

Is the punctuation correct? ☐

Compare the care

Elmtree House

Elmtree House offers traditional residential care, respite care and a caring residential environment for the elderly. Established in 1982, Elmtree House has an excellent reputation with all official bodies, doctors' surgeries and district nurses.

The experienced and highly qualified staff are committed to providing the best possible care to each and every resident. There have been no staff changes for a number of years and this underpins our success and the quality of care we provide.

We currently have both en suite and non en suite vacancies and look forward to assisting you with your enquiry.

Key facts

Registered care categories: Dementia • Old age

Single rooms: 18

Rooms with en suite WC: 8

Weekly charges guide: personal care single £390–£490 per week

Facilities and services: Day care • Respite care • Convalescent care • Physiotherapy • Independent living training • Own GP if required • Own furniture if required • Pets by arrangement • Smoking not permitted • Close to local shops • Near public transport • Minibus or other transport • Wheelchair access • Gardens for residents • Residents' kitchenette • Phone point in own room/ Mobile • Television point in own room

The Willows

The Willows is a warm, friendly and spacious care home with beautiful grounds to enjoy and a varied activities programme, which you can join in as little or as much as you like. This home was registered in 1964 and we offer longer stay, short stay and respite care as well as trial visits. Overnight visitors can usually be accommodated.

Residents may bring their own furniture and choose their room decoration. There is a lot of flexibility about meals. Activities are arranged daily. There are opportunities to pursue hobbies and to help with gardening.

Key facts

Conditions cared for: Older people generally

Single Rooms: 30

Rooms with en suite: 30

Cost: From £539 per week. Local Authority rates accepted

Facilities and services: Respite care • Sheltered housing • Own GP if required • Own furniture if required • Smoking not permitted • Close to local shops • Near public transport • Bus stop 0.25 mile; shop 0.25 mile; post office 0.25 mile; town centre 0.75 mile; GP 0.25 mile • Lift • Wheelchair access • Gardens for residents • Phone point in own room/Mobile • Television point in own room

A Read the text and answer these questions.

1 Who is this information aimed at?

2 Which home has been running the longest?

3 What is not allowed in either home?

4 Which home would you choose if you needed sheltered housing?

a) Elmtree House ☐

b) Neither home ☐

c) The Willows ☐

5 Where can residents have their own furniture in their room?

a) Elmtree House ☐

b) The Willows ☐

c) In both homes ☐

B Tick the name of the home that each statement refers to.

Statement	Elmtree House	The Willows
1 Residents can keep a pet.		
2 Activities are organised each day.		
3 It has a lift.		
4 There is a kitchen that residents can use.		

C Which of these statements are true and which are false?

1 Both homes are near a shop. True ☐ False ☐

2 Visitors can stay the night at Elmtree House. True ☐ False ☐

3 Residents can do gardening at The Willows. True ☐ False ☐

4 All of the rooms at Elmtree House are en suite. True ☐ False ☐

D Discuss the descriptions of the two homes with a partner.

- What differences do you notice in the style in which they are written?
- What effect does this have on the reader?
- Which home sounds most appealing and why?

Make notes about your discussion below.

E Suggest one thing about each home that you think could be a good selling point. Why would this appeal to people?

1 Elmtree House

Selling point:

Why it would appeal:

2 The Willows
Selling point:

Why it would appeal:

 F Tick whether the statements below are fact or opinion.

1 Staff turnover at Elmtree House is very low. Fact ☐ Opinion ☐

2 Keeping the same staff for many years has made Elmtree
House successful. Fact ☐ Opinion ☐

3 The Willows has beautiful gardens. Fact ☐ Opinion ☐

4 Residents can keep up their hobbies at The Willows. Fact ☐ Opinion ☐

G From your reading of the Elmtree House brochure, give two examples of how it might be biased.

1

2

H Write a positive description of a care home that will encourage people to find out more about it. It can be a home that you know or you can make one up.

Assistive technology

Assistive technology is technology used by individuals with disabilities in order to perform functions that might otherwise be difficult or impossible.

People with speech impairment might use a form of assistive technology known as augmentative and alternative communication (AAC). These are electronic devices that supplement or replace speech for people who are unable to speak, have difficulty speaking or whose speech is difficult to understand. They can use limited hand movements or even eye movements to make the device vocalise what they want to say.

The most famous person to use this type of technology to communicate is the British physicist Stephen Hawking, who suffers from motor neurone disease. AAC has allowed him to communicate, write and publish his works, and give lectures to live audiences around the world in spite of losing his ability to speak.

Communicating with someone who uses AAC

It can be daunting to meet someone for the first time when they use AAC, but it is important to remember that it is just another form of communication. Here are some tips for doing this in a sensitive manner:

- Face the person you are communicating with as you will be able to pick up visual clues such as gesture, facial expression and body language.
- It can be difficult for an AAC user to join into a conversation so ensure you invite questions or a response.
- Allow plenty of time for the AAC user to construct a message.
- Do not worry about silence when an AAC user is keying in. Talking during this process can distract them.
- Some users may mainly use preprogrammed messages so they have to use the 'best fit' message in response. Try to be creative in how you interpret these.
- AAC users can find long periods of using their communication aid tiring. If you sense this, give them a break.
- The AAC user has to rely on the vocabulary available in their communication device, which will be limited. Try to arrange for help so that they have the vocabulary they need installed on their device.

A Match each word to its meaning.

Word		Meaning	
1	Augmentative	a)	the lessening or absence of a mental or physical function
2	Impairment	b)	something that can act as a substitute
3	Assistive	c)	an addition to something to increase its size or make up for a deficiency
4	Supplement	d)	adding or increasing something or enabling it to increase
5	Alternative	e)	helping someone to do something

 B Read the text and answer these questions.

1 Who would use augmentative and alternative communication (AAC)?

2 When you are communicating with someone who uses AAC, why should you face them?

3 What condition does Stephen Hawking have?

4 How do people make an AAC device work for them?

5 Why should you not talk when an AAC user is keying in a message?

 C Discuss the following questions in your group.

• Who has seen someone using AAC?

• Has anyone worked with somebody who uses AAC?

• How might having AAC available help people psychologically?

• Do you think that people tend to treat individuals with speech impairments as if they are stupid?

• Why do you think this might be?

D Choose an appropriate word for each gap so that the sentences make sense.

1 It can be difficult for an AAC user to join in a [   ].

2 You need to be careful how you [   ] preprogrammed messages.

3 Give users a [   ] if they become tired.

4 Give the user plenty of [   ] to construct their message.

5 The vocabulary available on an AAC device will be [   ].

E Read about the conditions affecting speech below.

Conditions affecting speech	
Cerebral palsy	A wide-ranging condition that affects movement, posture and coordination. One of the main ways it affects people is a lack of muscle control, including the muscles involved in the production of speech.
Dysarthria	A speech disorder resulting from brain injury that is characterised by poor articulation.
Dysfluency	A speech disorder that results in hesitancies and stumbling (stammering) which can make speech difficult to understand.
Dysphasia	Impairment of language (especially speech production) that is usually due to brain damage.

You will have noticed that three of these conditions begin with 'dys'. This prefix means 'bad' or 'abnormal'. When it is used, it is almost always in medical or scientific words.

F Another prefix that sounds the same, but is spelt differently, is 'dis'. This is more common and simply makes the word negative, for example 'belief' and 'disbelief'.

Rewrite these statements to make them negative by adding 'dis' to one of the words.

1 I like Maggie.

[   ]

2 I trust Ian.

[   ]

3 David is quite a loyal person.

[   ]

H Reread the text about conditions that affect speech and choose the correct answer.

1 Which condition results in stammering?

a) Cerebral palsy ☐

b) Dysfluency ☐

c) Dysphasia ☐

2 Which condition affects the muscles involved in producing speech?

a) Dysarthria ☐

b) Dysfluency ☐

c) Cerebral palsy ☐

3 Which condition is characterised by poor articulation?

a) Dysarthria ☐

b) Dysfluency ☐

c) Dysphasia ☐

I Write a paragraph about why it is important to treat people who have speech impairment with respect.

FOCUS ON Conjunctions and prepositions

Conjunctions

You can use conjunctions to join two simple sentences together to make a longer, more interesting, sentence. For example:

- 'Mr Andrews has difficulty walking' is a simple sentence.
- 'He has arthritis' is also a simple sentence.

By joining them together with a conjunction we can make the sentence:

- 'Mr Andrews has difficulty walking because he has arthritis.'

A Choose from the common conjunctions below to join the following sentences together. In most cases there will be more than one option.

and   so   but   because   or   though   as

1   I like working at nights. It can be hard to adjust afterwards.

2   It is important to put paper waste in that bin. It can be recycled.

3   We organise a group activity every afternoon. Residents can get together and socialise.

4   The towels are stored in this cupboard. You will find the sheets in this one.

5   I would love to be a physiotherapist. I do not have the right qualifications.

6   Mrs White needs help with dressing. She is going to the hairdresser.

B Write a sentence containing one of these conjunctions.

provided that   as long as

Prepositions

You may not know the grammatical term 'preposition', but you will recognise these words and probably know how to use them. A preposition links nouns, pronouns and phrases to other words in a sentence.

C Choose from the prepositions below to fill the gaps in each sentence.

with   about   to   of   for   from

1   Bingo is very popular [   ] the residents.

2   We were all very sad [   ] Mr Singh's illness.

3   Jackie only eats free-range eggs because she is opposed [   ] factory farming.

4   I was not aware [   ] the health risks associated [   ] latex gloves.

5   Now I have been promoted I am responsible [   ] the induction [   ] new staff.

6   This day centre is completely different [   ] the one I was at before.

7   Off-job training is vital in order [   ] understand the theories in healthcare.

8   Working in care in Scotland is similar [   ] doing the same job in England.

D For each of the following phrases, write a sentence that contains the phrase.

pleased with   sorry about   intended for

1

2

3

FOCUS ON Writing an email

You may use email to keep in touch with friends or family – these are informal emails. Sometimes, however, you will have to write a **formal** email.

Formal emails are anything to do with your professional work, such as an email to a client's family or to another person you have to liaise with in health and social care. They also include emails relating to job applications or official organisations.

The tips below are very important for formal emails, but many of them apply to informal emails as well.

Top tips for writing effective emails

- Make sure you include something in the subject line. You would be amazed how many people forget to do this. If you are replying to an email you have received it may be all right to just keep the subject that is already there, but you need to decide whether you should change it.

- Write a clear and meaningful subject line. People often look at the subject line to decide whether to open or delete a message. Make sure the subject accurately describes the content. Do not put 'Important! Read Immediately' or 'Questions'.

- Think about how you will start the email. Although an email is more informal than a letter, if you are writing to someone for the first time and you do not know them, you should still write 'Dear xxx', not 'Hi'.

- Keep your message focused and readable. If you are making a number of points separate them with bullets, dashes or paragraphs.

- Use standard spelling and avoid shortening words as you might in a text message.

- Only use capitals where you should for correct grammar. Writing all in capitals can come across as SHOUTING!

- Even if you are complaining or angry about something, be polite. Harsh words can sound much ruder in an email.

- If you are writing to someone you do not know, include your full name and any other information they may need, such as a contact telephone number.

- Think about how you will end your email. In a formal letter you might write 'Yours sincerely' or 'Yours faithfully', but it has become common practice in email to end politely with 'Best regards' or 'Kind regards'.

- Read your email carefully before you send it. First read it to see how it sounds. Is the tone of voice right?

- Proofread your email for spelling mistakes or typos. Email may be a fast form of communication but that does not mean it should be rushed.

A Look at the email below.

Can you spot any mistakes? How could it be improved?

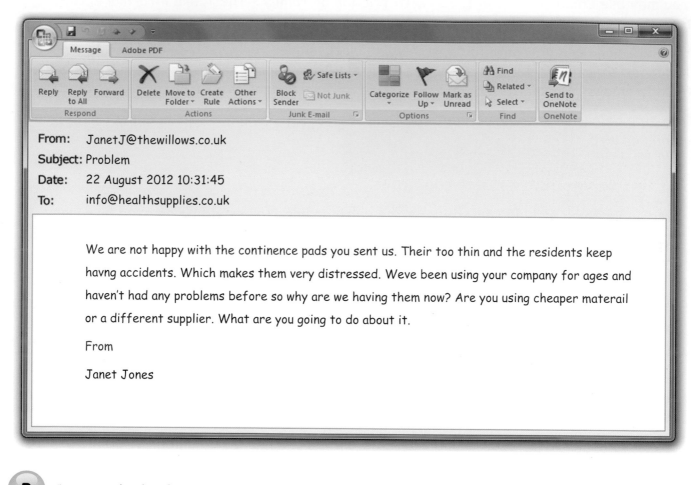

From: JanetJ@thewillows.co.uk

Subject: Problem

Date: 22 August 2012 10:31:45

To: info@healthsupplies.co.uk

We are not happy with the continence pads you sent us. Their too thin and the residents keep havng accidents. Which makes them very distressed. Weve been using your company for ages and haven't had any problems before so why are we having them now? Are you using cheaper materail or a different supplier. What are you going to do about it.

From

Janet Jones

B Can you think of times when you have had to write a formal email?

Share your examples in the group.

C Draft an email in reply to this job advert on a separate piece of paper. Use the checklist of tips to help you and check your draft when you have finished.

> **Vacancy for care assistant**
>
> Elmtree House has a vacancy for an enthusiastic and hardworking care assistant in our successful residential home. We are looking for a Healthcare Assistant who has experience in either a hospital or community setting within the UK. For further details and to apply please email Mrs Barbara West at Bwest@elmtree.co.uk

FOCUS ON Writing a formal letter

Elements of a formal letter

Formal letters include letters that you write in your work, letters for job applications, letters of complaint, and so on. When you write formal letters you include these required elements:

- Your own address or the name, address and phone number of your organisation go at the top of the letter. Many organisations use headed notepaper so there is no need to type in the address.

- The name and address of the person you are writing to go next, on the left-hand side of the page, followed by the date.

- The 'salutation' comes next, which can be Dear Sir/Madam, Dear Mr/Mrs [surname], or Dear [first name] if you know the person well.

- It is then common to include the subject of the letter or a reference (e.g. 'Re your letter of 5 May 2012').

- You then write the letter, broken into paragraphs.

- If you greeted the recipient by name, you should finish the letter with 'Yours sincerely' followed by your signature and name. If you began with 'Dear Sir/Madam', you should end with 'Yours faithfully'.

For example:

Home from home
Park Crescent
Manchester M23 4LS
Phone: 0161 123 4567

Mr Ben Simmons
25 Hincham Lane
Manchester M23 1LB

16 September 2012

Dear Mr Simmons

Sponsored walk

I am writing to thank you for taking part in the sponsored walk in aid of the Home from Home appeal.

In total we were able to raise £2,415 from the sponsored walk, which will go towards the refurbishment of the day room.

Once again, I am most grateful for your time and support.

Yours sincerely

Jane Lawton

Managing Director

A Put the required elements of a formal letter in the correct order from the top to the bottom of the page by numbering each point.

- Your address
- Your name and/or position
- Subject of the letter or reference
- Your signature
- The correct closing phrase (Yours ...)
- The date
- The name and address of the person you are writing to
- The salutation (Dear ...)

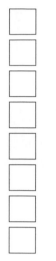

Structure of the letter

The main content of the letter is likely to include the following:

- An introductory paragraph – this may thank the reader for an earlier letter or introduce you and explain why you are writing.

- Main paragraphs – these will set out the point(s) you want to make. Each point should have its own paragraph.

- A closing paragraph – you may end by summing up what you have said, proposing next steps or saying 'I look forward to hearing from you.'

Always use formal language, avoiding slang, abbreviations and jargon.

Checking what you have written

Next time you write a formal letter, use this checklist:

- Have you included all of the required elements (names, addresses, date, salutation and closing elements)?
- Have you used headed notepaper if available?
- Is the reason you are writing clear?
- Is the tone of your writing polite and businesslike?
- Have you used appropriate language?
- Have you explained why you are writing?
- Does each main point or idea have its own paragraph?
- Is everything easy to understand?
- Is it clear what will happen next?
- Is your spelling, punctuation and grammar correct?